REASONS
TO
STAY

Jusu Kamara

Studio of Books LLC
5900 Balcones Drive Suite 100
Austin, Texas 78731
www.studioofbooks.org
Hotline: (254) 800-1183

Ordering Information:
Special discounts are available on quantity purchases by corporations, associations, and others. For details, contact the publisher at the address above.

Printed in the United States of America.

ISBN-13: Softcover   978-1-964928-55-5
          eBook   978-1-964928-56-2

Library of Congress Control Number: 2025909647

TABLE *of* CONTENTS

PREFACE

The journey of life is often unpredictable, marked by moments of joy and peace that can swiftly be interrupted by unimaginable tragedy.

My story began in a place I once called paradise: Margibi County, Liberia, in the vibrant and beautiful West Africa, not far from the borders of Sierra Leone and Ivory Coast. It was a place where my family and I lived in harmony, surrounded by the warmth of community and love.

We lived through the typical days of a happy childhood, blissfully unaware of the dark clouds gathering on the horizon. My father and mother, like many Liberian parents, made sure that every holiday season was special, filled with laughter and love. We were raised to be good children, and we lived a life that seemed as peaceful as any child's could be, far removed from the hardships that others faced.

Our daily lives revolved around school, playing with friends, and enjoying the carefree nature of youth in a place where danger seemed a distant thought.

But everything changed when Charles Taylor sought to unseat Samuel Doe, igniting a civil war that would tear apart our nation. Overnight, Liberia was plunged into chaos, and we found ourselves in the crosshairs of a conflict we barely understood.

This story revolves around the harrowing journey my family and I endured as our world crumbled around us. It speaks of our strength in the face of tyranny, the tragedies we encountered, and the losses we suffered. Yet, it also reflects the resilience and determination we found amid the chaos.

Our journey from Liberia to the United States was long and fraught with danger, but it had moments of hope and triumph. The challenges I faced along the way shaped the man I became.

I share this story not just as a recounting of my past but as a beacon of hope for others who may face their own battles, whatever form they may take. Through it all, I learned that life's greatest challenges can also be the source of our greatest strength. Now, I hold onto the belief that, "The race is not to the swift, but to those who endure to the end."

This is my story, and I invite you all to explore the power of endurance, resilience, and hope with me.

Chapter 1

BEST TIME

Settled on the west coast of Africa, Liberia is a country adorned with stunning natural beauty and a unique cultural heritage. Back when the land wasn't plagued with war and crime, Liberia used to be a breathtaking haven for its residents. It had a serene vibe, with air that compelled you to breathe in the freedom it had. I still remember how content it felt to step out of the house an breathe the air that didn't wreak of war, filth, or crime. Life seemed so simple, so at ease that we couldn't even dream that one day we'd be trying to escape our beautiful home.

Liberia shares its borders with Sierra Leone to the northwest, Guinea to the north, and Côte d'Ivoire to the east, with the Atlantic Ocean stretching along its southwestern coast. Now, you can imagine the beauty it held. Everywhere you looked, every way you went held so much promise of exquisiteness that your heart would rejoice at the very sight of it.

It wouldn't be wrong to say that the country was a masterpiece of a land that had no other match. You may think that I'm biased because it was my country but it really was the undeniable truth.

The West African geography wore this beautiful land with pride, expressing its dense rainforests, vast savannas, and an expansive coastline that directly connects to the crashing waves of the Atlantis.

You might think the beachy vibes may attract the onlookers, but in all honesty, it was the lush greenery that set Liberia apart. The rolling hills and mountain were the epitome of magnificence that complements the country's vibrant culture.

Every time you hear about Liberia, you'll stumble upon Margibi County in every conversation. There is no way that you talk about Liberia and not discuss Margibi County. It is located near the central region of the country and has numerous picturesque spots that will surely mesmerize you. And you know what's the best part? It is not far from the capital city of Monrovia. You can have the best of both worlds, the bustling life of the urban and the scenic escape from it. Roads are lined with palms and the air is filled with cool breezes.

What used to stun my young mind was the deep red soil of the countryside something that aptly represent Liberia. Another thing that I couldn't believe was how the lush rainforests and rivers snake their way through the county, creating a backdrop for what seemed to be a peaceful existence for its residents. All in all, it was beauty, serene, and most importantly, safe– deemed worthy to be called home. Oh, how I loved it!

Things started going south without any of us realizing what has happened. I was just a kid when it all began, living with my father, oblivious to the horrors of the world. To me, our home was a haven that fostered dreams and daily shenanigans. We were all very happy, leading an ordinary life that seemed extraordinary to my young mind. Every day, without fail, I would wake up early in the morning with birds chirping over my head. The soft rustling of leaves would welcome me, blowing through the trees. To my wondrous self, it seemed like a tranquil life that I wanted to enjoy.

Liberia was an unspoiled land brimming with hope before the civil unrest tore the country apart. Even though it had always been a target point, thanks to the political unrest, but it had never seen destruction. Before I dive into my story, let me tell you a little background of the political situation of Liberia.

Founded by freed African-American slaves in the 19th century, Liberia was unique in its historical context. It was Africa's first and only republic established by free African-Americans, and this distinction placed it on a pedestal of sorts. However, this did not shield the country from the tensions brewing underneath.

For decades, Liberia was ruled by a small elite descended from the original settlers, also known as Americo-Liberians. This created a division between the Americo-Liberians and the indigenous people, who made up the majority of the population. The long-standing tensions between these two groups bubbled beneath the surface as the country modernized and sought to define itself post – independence. Despite Liberia's rich cultural heritage, its political scene was marred by inequality and corruption.

In the 1980s, Samuel Doe, a native Liberian, took control of the country through a military coup, ending the long rule of the Americo – Liberian elite descendants of freed American slaves. Many hoped Doe would bring change and fairness to Liberia and make life better for the native population. At first, he seemed like a hero. But soon, his government turned into a harsh dictatorship. Corruption flourished, and the economy suffered. People faced political oppression and favoritism based on ethnicity, which drove deeper divides in the country. As discontent grew, the stage was set for conflict.

The spark that ignited the flames of war came with Charles Taylor, a former government official under Doe. Accused of stealing money, Taylor fled to the United States but returned to Liberia in 1989 with a militia called the National Patriotic Front of Liberia (NPFL). His goal was clear: to overthrow Doe.

Taylor launched his insurgency in northern Liberia, and the violence spread quickly. Doe's forces responded with brutality and the fighting escalated. What began as a political struggle turned into a conflict that engulfed the entire nation. These episodes of political unrest did not care about anyone or anything; all they knew was the hunger of power. They paid no heed to the general populace and stretched the conflict to another level, where every citizen paid the price of a crime they didn't commit. Communities were torn apart, and a humanitarian crisis unfolded. The devastation of the country was brimming, but nobody paid any heed to anything. All they cared about was winning. The negligence and disregard escalated quickly, which led to devastating consequences for countless lives.

As the war dragged on, new factions emerged, alliances shifted, and the chaos only grew. They kept on putting up a picture that we are doing this for the country; however, that was clearly not the case.

Liberia was plunged into a cycle of violence quicker than anyone would ever imagine. When it all started, nobody knew that this unending streak of violence would leave deep scars on the mind of the countless. These scars forever changed the country and its people; nobody ever knew peace after this. Some people had hope that it would end in the near future; however, the hopes were crushed and it was clear that a united future was a distant dream. This dream was replaced by a grim reality where survival was the only priority. Nobody cared about the country then; they were all only concerned about their own survival.

Before the civil unrest disrupted our lives, my world was centered around my father. He was a man of remarkable integrity, somebody who didn't rest until his family was taken care of. He was a conservator by profession, working with the local natural resources and land, making sure that both nature and our livelihoods were preserved for future generations. It was a job that not only sustained our family but also reflected his deep-rooted values of hard work, honesty, and stewardship. He was a man who lived simply but with great purpose, and his influence extended beyond our household to our neighbors and the community at large.

My father was the kind of man who made an impression on everyone he met. His quiet strength, combined with an undeniable kindness, earned him the respect and admiration of our community. People often came to him for advice or a helping hand, knowing that he would always find time to assist them, no matter how busy he was. He believed in giving without expecting anything in return a value that he passed on to each of his children.

His work ethic was unmatched. My siblings and I often watched in awe as he tackled the challenges of his job, working long hours under the scorching African sun to ensure that our family was provided for. Yet, despite his busy schedule, he never failed to make time for us. Whether it was fixing something around the house, helping with homework, or simply sitting down to talk, my father was always present. His warmth filled every corner of our home, and his dedication to our well-being was the foundation upon which our family's happiness was built.

My mother was the heart of our household, her presence felt in every corner of our lives. With her boundless energy, she orchestrated our daily routines with grace. Breakfasts were never rushed, as she took the time to prepare warm meals that filled our home with delightful aromas, ensuring we started our day nourished and ready. After breakfast, she would meticulously tidy the house, transforming it into a haven of order.

Sometimes, I would be amazed at her dedication towards her family. She was a multitasker, managing everyone and everything with such grace and precision that it would blow my mind. How could one person do so much, I used to wonder. But then, I guess they are right when they say that a mother's love knows no bound; it's the purest form of love. And indeed, it is.

When I was a kid, I used to think that she was like the sun. Her love like its warmth, ready to greet us each morning, illuminating our lives with hope and encouragement. She made sure we were always prepared for the day, laying out our clothes, her gentle reminders echoing in our minds long after we left home. Evenings were filled with laughter and stories, as we gathered around the table, sharing the highlights of our day. My mother listened intently, her eyes sparkling with pride at our achievements and her heart heavy during our struggles. She taught us the importance of community, resilience, and the power of love.

For me and my siblings, daily life revolved around school and play. We attended a local school, where we were taught by strict but caring teachers who instilled in us the importance of education. My father, in particular, emphasized the value of learning. He would always tell us, "Education is your key to a better future," and we took his words to heart. We tried our best to make our parents proud, always ready to put in the work.

School was not just a place for academic learning but also for developing friendships and participating in various activities. When we weren't studying, my siblings and I spent hours playing outdoors. The natural beauty of Margibi County provided the perfect playground. We climbed trees, swam in nearby rivers, and played soccer in open fields with other children from the neighborhood.

Those were the carefree days of our childhood, where the biggest worry we had was whether we would win our next game.

We had a pretty great, peaceful life Lin Margibi County. I couldn't help but feel a profound sense of order and routine, a comforting rhythm to our days that I didn't know I'd be missing for the rest of my days. We had a modest house, cozy enough for all of us. To the outside world, it would be congested or small, but to us, it was a sanctuary, surrounded by friendly neighbors who felt more like extended family. We had close-knit community that thrived on connection; everyone knew each other, sharing in both our joys and challenges. Whether it was celebrating a neighbor's birthday or coming together during tough times, the spirit of love and consideration made every day a little easier.

The sense of community in Margibi was unlike anything I've experienced since. During the holiday seasons, especially, our home would be filled with laughter and joy as neighbors and family gathered to celebrate. My parents were known for their generosity, often hosting parties where everyone was welcome. My father, in particular, had a remarkable gift for making everyone feel special. He had a way of transforming even the simplest interactions into memorable moments. I marveled at how he used to infuse every interaction with warmth and genuine interest. Whether it was a neighbor stopping by for a chat or a distant relative visiting for the holidays, his kindness and hospitality were evident in every gesture.

When neighbors came by, my father would greet them with a broad smile and a hearty handshake, instantly putting them at ease. He had an uncanny ability to remember the little details like the name of their child or the last time they discussed the weather making each conversation feel personal and meaningful. He would listen intently, his eyes sparkling with curiosity as he asked about their lives, offering advice when needed and laughter when appropriate. In his presence, even the most mundane topics came alive. He had a sense of camaraderie that brightened our community.

During the holidays, our home transformed into a welcoming haven for family and friends. My father would spend hours preparing for their arrival, ensuring that the house was filled with warmth and the tantalizing aromas of his favorite dishes. As relatives arrived, he would greet them at the door with open arms, making each person feel like the guest of honor. His infectious laughter filled the rooms, and stories from his past would flow freely, drawing everyone into a shared narrative that connected us all.

He had a unique talent for creating a sense of belonging. At family gatherings, he would encourage everyone to share their stories, ensuring that even the quietest voices were heard. His ability to build connections was not limited to our home; it rippled through the community, bringing people together in ways that made them feel valued and appreciated.

My father's kindness extended beyond just our immediate circle; he often volunteered his time to help those in need, whether it was assisting a neighbor with repairs or organizing community events. He taught us that hospitality was not just about sharing food and drink, but about creating a space where everyone felt welcome and loved.

His dedication to kindness became a foundation of our family values. He instilled in us a deep appreciation for the power of connection and the importance of nurturing relationships. Through his example, we learned that making others feel special is one of the simplest yet most profound ways to enrich our lives and the lives of those around us.

Everything was going great, until it wasn't. As children, we were blissfully unaware of the political tensions simmering in the background. Life felt perfect. We had a loving family, a stable home, and the freedom to explore the beauty of the world, or so it seemed. It was an unimaginable thing for us that this peace could ever be disturbed. But in hindsight, there were subtle signs that change was on the horizon.

I recall overhearing conversations between my father and other adults, discussions about the government and the growing unrest in the country. My father, though always optimistic, began to show signs of concern. He was a man who believed in the goodness of people, but even he could sense that Liberia was heading toward a period of great uncertainty.

For us children, however, the days leading up to the civil unrest were filled with nothing but joy. We had no concept of war, no understanding of the forces that were about to turn our world upside down. Instead, we focused on the simple pleasures of life school, play, and spending time with family. The innocence of those days is something I hold onto dearly, even as the memories of the war loom large in my mind.

As the conflict between Charles Taylor and Samuel Doe escalated, our peaceful life in Margibi County began to unravel. At first, it was subtle a hushed conversation at the market, a fleeting news report on the radio. Whispers of violence from distant regions, murmurs of skirmishes near the border, were easily dismissed. We carried on with our daily routines, clinging to the familiar rhythm of life that had enveloped us for so long. But the tension in the air grew thicker, like a storm cloud gathering on the horizon, and soon, the reality of war would come crashing into our lives, shattering the tranquility we had once taken for granted.

It started with unsettling nights, the distant sounds of gunfire and explosions echoing through the valleys, unsettling our sleep and casting a shadow over our days. Conversations that had once been filled with laughter turned somber, and the smiles of our neighbors were tinged with worry. Families began to discuss evacuation plans, and the vibrant community gatherings we once cherished were replaced with anxious whispers and furtive glances. The very fabric of our close-knit community began to fray.

One evening, as the sun dipped below the horizon, we gathered around the dinner table. My father spoke softly, trying to reassure us, but his voice carried an undercurrent of concern that we could all feel. The clattering of utensils seemed louder than usual, and even the food, which my mother had lovingly prepared, felt heavy in our mouths. We were aware that our world was changing, and the innocence of our childhood was slipping away.

News from the outside world became more alarming with each passing day. Families in neighboring villages began to flee, their eyes wide with fear as they recounted the horrors they had witnessed.

They spoke of homes burned to the ground, loved ones lost, and a life turned upside down. The stories hung in the air like a thick fog, suffocating our sense of security. We could no longer ignore the impending storm, and the weight of uncertainty pressed down on us.

As the violence crept closer, we found ourselves grappling with the fear of what might come next. My parents worked tirelessly to protect us, trying to maintain a semblance of normalcy, but the anxiety was palpable. We could hear the distant rumblings of conflict, and with each passing day, it became clearer that the peace we had taken for granted was slipping through our fingers. The vibrant community we had cherished began to feel like a fragile shell, teetering on the brink of collapse, and we were left to wonder how much longer we could hold on to the life we once knew.

The Liberia I knew before the civil war was a land of beauty, promise, and simplicity. My family thrived in the peaceful community of Margibi County, where we were surrounded by natural splendor and a supportive network of friends and neighbors. But beneath the surface, the seeds of conflict had already been sown, and the storm that was about to engulf our country would forever change the course of our lives.

Chapter 2

———— ❧ ————

Introduction to Destruction

When the Civil War started, we were shaken beyond measure. But it happened so fast that we barely had time to express our shock or process what was happening. Our lives were getting uprooted, and there was nothing we could do. Not just us; it was a brutal conflict that tore the entire country apart. It officially began on December 24, 1989. The world might know this date as the initiation of this war; however, the true war started way before December 24. The seeds of this war had been sown years earlier through political mismanagement, economic instability, ethnic tensions, and the aspirations of one man, Charles Taylor, to seize power.

It was a terrible time, and those who have experienced it know it. This period in Liberia's history was nothing but filled with atrocities and brutalities. The nation's social and political fabric unraveled as years of authoritarian rule under President Samuel Doe and the rising ambitions of Charles Taylor led to one of Africa's deadliest conflicts.

Before I dip my feet in and tell you about my life and the atrocities I personally felt due to this war, let me explain the concept of this war to those of you who are unfamiliar with it. In order to understand the effects of the war, it is important to learn about its background. It stretches all the way back to 1980 when Master Sergeant Samuel Doe, a young soldier from the Krahn ethnic group, led a coup d'état that overthrew the government of President William Tolbert. This coup ended the AmericoLiberian dominance that had been in place since the country's founding in 1847. The Americo-Liberians were descendants of freed slaves from the United States who had settled in Liberia and maintained political and economic control for over a century.

When Samuel Doe rose to power, it was the first time that the natives took the reigns of their government. Initially, this sudden change was welcomed with open arms. Everyone was optimistic on the surface; however, inwardly, the general populace was somewhat cautious of the sudden changes that have been happening in the country. They did not know what to expect and how it would pan out for their futures and that of their children.

And eventually, their apprehensive cautiousness proved to be right because the rule that seemed free at first very soon turned into authoritarianism. Why, you ask? Because corruption took root in the hearts of those who were supposed to protect the country from it.

Favoritism was at its peak, and there was a prevalent abuse of power and human rights that nobody seemed to shake. The government was notorious for its persecution of opposition members, and as time passed, his regime became increasingly ethnocentric. It would only favor his own Krahn tribe and marginalize others, particularly the Gio and Mano ethnic groups in northern Liberia. Tribal tensions were rearing their heads as discord emerged before anyone could imagine. These tribal tensions became a crucial factor in the descent into civil war.

By the mid-1980s, Doe had put a mark on his power through a mix of repression and constitutional manipulation. It is said that he ensured his presidency by rigging the 1985 elections. When that happened, nobody said anything. The international community, particularly the United States, supported Doe because they viewed him as a bulwark against the spread of communism in West Africa during the Cold War. Everything seemed hunky dory for him, and he thought he'd made it.

However, when his regime became brutal and unstable, there was no saving him. This is because international support eventually waned. Seeing this, those who were opposed to his government and disliked his way of being eventually decided to fight back; hence, internal opposition began to grow. Ethnic groups that felt sidelined by Doe's favoritism toward the Krahn began organizing against him. Liberia's condition worsened. It was already one of the poorest nations in the world, so its deteriorating state was alarming and beyond measure. When economic mismanagement, corruption, and repression became too hard to handle, chaos reigned.

It was time for an intervention. It was time for a change. It was time to change the dynamics of the country. Enter Charles Taylor, a charismatic figure who would become one of Africa's most infamous warlords. Born in 1948, Taylor studied in the United States. Even though he spent a significant amount of time there, he decided to return to Liberia in the 1980s to work for Doe's government. Things worked well in the initial days of his career, but it all unraveled when he was accused of embezzling nearly $1 million from the government.

Upon receiving these allegations, Taylor fled to the US, only to be arrested and held in a Massachusetts jail. He later escaped under mysterious circumstances, allegedly with CIA assistance, and made his way to Libya, where he received military training and formed alliances with other African insurgent groups. In Libya, Taylor became associated with Muammar Gaddafi, who was keen on spreading his influence across Africa by supporting rebel movements. Taylor found ideological and financial support from Gaddafi, which he used to found the National Patriotic Front of Liberia (NPFL) in 1989. Taylor's goal was clear: to topple Samuel Doe and take control of Liberia.

On December 24, 1989, Taylor and a small force of NPFL rebels, many of them Gio and Mano fighters from Liberia's marginalized north, crossed the border from Côte d'Ivoire into Liberia. This was the official beginning of the Liberian Civil War. Taylor's initial incursion into Liberia was not seen as a serious threat by the Doe regime, but within months, his forces had grown and began capturing significant portions of the countryside. Taylor's strategy was to incite ethnic hatred against the Krahn and Mandingo groups, using long-standing grievances to gain popular support.

Ethnic tensions were a major underlying cause of the civil war. As mentioned earlier, Doe had heavily favored his own Krahn ethnic group during his rule. He gave them key positions in the military and government. This favoritism alienated other groups, particularly the Gio and Mano tribes, who had suffered under Doe's rule. When Taylor's forces entered Liberia, they played on these ethnic divisions, portraying the NPFL as liberators of the oppressed Gio and Mano people.

The NPFL's campaign quickly became an ethnically driven war. Taylor's forces targeted Krahn and Mandingo civilians, leading to widespread massacres and atrocities. In response, Krahn militias and other groups loyal to Doe retaliated, leading to a cycle of violence that spiraled out of control. Entire villages were wiped out, and tens of thousands of civilians were displaced or killed. The brutality of the war, with its widespread use of child soldiers and systematic violence against civilians, shocked the world.

As Taylor's NPFL continued its assault, Doe's grip on power weakened. By mid-1990, the Liberian capital, Monrovia, was under siege, with various rebel factions controlling large parts of the country. Amid the chaos, a splinter group from the NPFL, the Independent National Patriotic Front of Liberia (INPFL), led by Prince Johnson, emerged. Johnson, a former ally of Taylor, had become disillusioned with Taylor's leadership and sought power for himself.

The situation in Monrovia became dire as the INPFL and NPFL battled for control of the capital while government forces loyal to Doe tried to hold out. Meanwhile, Doe's regime was crumbling from within, as many of his soldiers deserted, and his ability to command effectively deteriorated. Ethnic violence was rampant, and Monrovia became the epicenter of the conflict, with civilians caught in the crossfire.

Then, things took a drastic turn in Liberia's history. As time passed, things did not work in Doe's favor as he was captured by Prince Johnson's INPFL at the headquarters of Economic Community of West African States Monitoring Group (ECOMOG). It was a regional peacekeeping force that wanted to intervene and stabilize the situation, and they proved to be dependable in this situation.

And mind you, things didn't end there. It was said that when he was captured, he was brutally tortured for days. Eventually, they decided to execute him. Things were in an uproar as his regime ended quite brutally. It was thought that with his end, the political situation of the country would get better. However, no such thing happened. In fact, the hostility intensified, and people from various factions jumped in to fight for control of the country.

One prominent thing that came out of Doe's death was Taylor's eager enthusiasm to reign over Liberia. He thought he would have no hurdles in his way. However, ECOMOG intervened again and thwarted his efforts. It favored a transitional government and established a buffer zone in Monrovia in the hopes of bringing peace to the country. But Taylor wasn't the one to back down easily; he wasn't the one to let go without a fight; he wasn't the one to compromise. Hence, he continued his war against the interim government without caring about the time and effort that was required. The conflict was nowhere near solved with Doe's death; in fact, it stretched on for years.

Taylor wasn't stupid to have fought all those years, as most people think. He had control over the countryside, which allowed him to exploit Liberia's natural resources. He didn't care about anything; he caught hold of timber, rubber, and diamonds and utilized them for his financial gains. That's how he funded his war efforts as well. He was inconsiderate, ruthless, and brutal, to say the least. He used to employ heinous tactics to keep himself afloat and maintain his grip on power. His atrocities were the talk of the town, and it is said that he didn't think twice before indulging in mass murders, rapes, and forced conscription of children.

The civil war continued for seven more years as various factions fought for control. Initially, it seemed like there was no end to it. All it brought was immense human suffering. By the time peace was finally brokered in 1997, over 200,000 Liberians had been killed, and nearly half of the population had been displaced. Liberia's infrastructure was in ruins, and the social fabric of the country had been torn apart.

In 1997, Charles Taylor, despite his role in prolonging the war, was elected president in a controversial election that many believed was influenced by fear and intimidation. However, Taylor's rule brought little peace to Liberia at least for a while. However, the so-called peace did not last, and the country descended into a second civil war in 1999, which lasted until his eventual ouster in 2003.

The Liberian Civil War was the result of a complex mix of ethnic tensions, political instability, and the personal ambitions of men like Charles Taylor. Samuel Doe's corrupt and divisive regime created the conditions for rebellion, and Taylor's NPFL exploited these weaknesses to launch a brutal insurgency. What began as a quest for power soon devolved into a humanitarian catastrophe, with the civilian population bearing the brunt of the violence. The legacy of the war continues to affect Liberia to this day, as the country still grapples with the scars left by years of conflict, ethnic division, and economic ruin. The civil war serves as a grim reminder of the dangers of unchecked ambition, authoritarianism, and the destructive power of ethnic hatred.

To this day, I can feel the horrors of the war. To my young mind, the first place that seemed real, that I could call home, that I felt safe during those times of horror was my mother's house in Gardnersville, Montserrado Country. It wasn't a fancy place; it had small homes and modest businesses that would attract no one in today's day and age. But then, it was a haven for us. Even though the occasional car rumbled down the dirt roads, we didn't mind the dust that settled on the lust trees around our house. We were at peace there, enjoying the quiet, slow-moving life of the area.

If you think that it didn't look like much of an attraction, you may be right. But hear me out when I say that it was the only place that a frightened little kid like me could call home during the war. In fact, it was my favorite way before the war began. It held innate simplicity that seemed to capture my heart every time I visited. It was a part of the capital, Monrovia, but not as much as it would attract unnecessary political upheaval. Yet, to the best of my knowledge, it was close enough to the capital that we all felt connected to the pulse of the country.

This place seemed like a perfect little sanctuary if we had to get away from the busyness of life. All of us family members would go there to seek the much-needed moments of peace and quiet whenever we had time. Little did I know that we would have to treat it as a literal sanctuary amidst the horrors of the war. Before the war, it was a place to escape; however, when the war erupted, it became nothing but a place of survival.

After that, nothing seemed the same. Everything changed, never to be reverted to normal. The first rumblings of the rebellions reached us with the stories of Charles Taylor's fighters who were wreaking all over the place blatantly. They were sweeping through the northern and eastern parts of Liberia without having any regard or mercy for the residents. Forget residents; they even killed government officials without fear. They didn't stop at the killings; they looted villages and targeted everyone who didn't side with them, especially the ethnic groups that were against their reign of terror.

Unfortunately, my father worked for the government that did not favor the reigning troops. We were afraid that sooner or later, he would become the target, and our fears were realized sooner than we thought. The rebels, knowing his position in the government, marked him for execution, wanting his blood at any cost. Initially, we were skeptical about the immediate threat to his life, not understanding the real reason. To our knowledge, just holding a government position would not make him an immediate target. There had to be another reason, and there was!

Our family name was a huge issue we didn't know we had. "Kamara" connected us, however distantly, to the Mandingo tribe, which became such an issue for us because it was a group they singled out for extermination due to tribalism and the perceived alignment with the ruling government. So, the moment they got to know about my father's family name, they became hungry for his blood. The situation became so precarious that the future of our family seemed bleak at best. It felt like his very existence was a threat to them, to us, to the future of our family.

We were really scared that we would have to say goodbye to our father, whose only fault was having a surname people had issues with. The outbreak of violence was terrifying, to say the least, and we had to do something to protect my father. He realized the gravity of the situation and knew what he had to do to save his neck. We decided to leave Margibi County and find a new place to hide, a place where every one of us was safe. And we had to do it fast. Any moment spent there was like getting closer to committing suicide.

There have been certain instances in my life that I still remember very vividly. Even though I was a kid, there was nothing that I remember more clearly than the terrifying look on my father's face. One thing that was even more unsettling was the glint of worry in his eyes for his family member. He knew that the rebels were ruthless, and he couldn't bear the thought of putting his family in harm's way. He thought it was his fault that were all in danger, but the truth was, even without his association with the government or the name he harbored, every person was getting the brunt of the rebel's group. They only needed an excuse to execute their killings, and we were no exception.

After a thoughtful discussion, we decided to leave the town as soon as possible. We packed whatever we could, making sure our sacks were as light as possible, and went on our way. Since we didn't have the luxury to make pitstops or wait for anyone or anything, we had to carry light. My father, who was an ultimate family, couldn't bear the thought of leaving us, but he had no other choice. We left Margibi County and went on to Gardnersville. He knew if he moved with us, he would be recognized, and the consequences would be dire. Therefore, we stayed back, hoping that his absence would take the heat off our family. All he wanted was to give us a chance at safety.

The journey to Gardnersville was tense. We traveled with a group of neighbors, all fleeing the fighting. Every sound a twig breaking in the forest, the distant hum of an engine, even birds taking off into the sky made our hearts race. We didn't know who might be watching or if we would be stopped by rebels demanding to know who we were. My father had warned us to be careful with our last name. Kamara, as common as it might be in other contexts, had become a death sentence. I was too young to grasp the gravity of that truth fully, but I could sense the fear in my mother's eyes every time someone asked us who we were or where we were going.

When we finally reached Gardnersville, it was a relief, though not the kind of relief one might expect. The area was safer than where we had come from, but it was not untouched by the war. When we reached there, I had a hard time recognizing the streets that used to be so full of life. I remembered how lively they used to be, with children playing and people going about their daily routines. Now, every street I stepped on, everywhere we looked, felt deserted. There was an eerie quiet to the place.

One thing that seemed weird to me was the absence of men in those streets. Most of them were gone. Some had joined the rebels, others had fled, and many had already been killed. There was something so sinister, so eerily quiet in the air, something that gave us the creeps. My mother's house, which once felt like a warm, inviting space, now felt like a fortress filled with solitude. Even though we were living there, there was a solitary gloom that seemed to fill the air. The windows were boarded up, and the doors were bolted shut, not to keep out animals or thieves but to protect us from the war.

My young, terrified heart could neither understand nor bear the gloom that had immediately settled into our lives. Life in Gardnersville under the shadow of war was a constant reminder that things can change at any given moment. It was a balancing act between hope and fear, for we were constantly afraid, with a small hope brimming in our hearts that one day, everything might get back to normal.

My mother was strong, stronger than I could have ever imagined. She kept us calm, even when we could hear gunfire in the distance or when news reached us of someone we knew being killed. She never let on how scared she was, but I could see it in the way her hands trembled when she thought we weren't looking or how her voice shook just slightly when she told us everything would be okay.

Our daily routine shifted into one of survival. We spent most of our time inside, avoiding any attention. Outside, the streets were no longer safe. Rebels and looters had taken over parts of the town, and they were suspicious of anyone they didn't recognize. There were constant rumors of people being dragged out of their homes and executed. The tribalism that had once been simmering beneath the surface of Liberian society had exploded into open violence, and it was tearing the country apart.

I remember the day the rebels came to Gardnersville. It was early morning, just after dawn, when we first heard the trucks rumbling down the road. We knew instantly what it meant. My mother gathered us in the back room, away from the windows, and told us to be quiet. We could hear the shouting outside as the rebels made their way through the neighborhood, kicking down doors and pulling people out into the streets. We sat huddled together, trying to make ourselves as small as possible. My mother held us close, whispering prayers under her breath.

They came to our house, banging on the door and demanding to be let in. My heart was pounding so hard I thought they would hear it. My mother didn't move, didn't make a sound. We waited, barely breathing, as the rebels tried to break down the door. For a moment,

I thought they would get in, that this was the end. But then, as suddenly as they had arrived, they were gone, moving on to the next house. We waited for what felt like hours before we dared to move, and then my mother finally let out the breath she had been holding.

After that day, things in Gardnersville got worse. The rebels had taken over parts of the town, and the violence escalated. People disappeared regularly, either taken by the rebels or simply fleeing into the wilderness, hoping to find safety elsewhere. Food became scarce, and water even more so. My mother would go out early in the morning to try and find food for us, always coming back with less than she had hoped for. There were days when we went hungry, days when we didn't know if we would make it through to the next.

In the midst of all this, we still held on to some semblance of normalcy. My mother made sure we kept up with our studies, even though school was out of the question. She found old books, whatever she could get her hands on, and made us read. It was her way of keeping our minds sharp, of reminding us that there was a world beyond the war, a future that we could still hope for.

But the war was always there, lurking just outside our door. One night, the fighting came too close for comfort. We could hear the gunfire and explosions, the screams of people running for their lives. My mother didn't wait this time. She gathered us up, and we fled, running through the streets of Gardnersville in the dead of night and dodging the chaos around us. We made it to a church on the outskirts of town, where other families had gathered for refuge. It wasn't much, but it was safer than staying in the house. The church became our new home for a while, a place where we could at least feel a little safer.

The days at the church blurred together. We were surrounded by people just like us, people who had lost everything but were clinging to the hope that the war would end and that life would return to normal. There were moments of joy, small victories like finding food or water or hearing that a family member had survived. But there were also moments of despair, like when someone didn't come back or when we heard that the rebels had taken another town.

As the war dragged on, Gardnersville became more and more isolated. The roads were cut off, and communication with the outside world was nearly impossible. We had no way of knowing what was happening in other parts of the country, no way of knowing if my father was still alive. The uncertainty was the hardest part. Every day, I wondered if he had made it, if he had found a way to survive. My mother tried to stay optimistic, but I could see the doubt in her eyes.

After months of living in Gardnersville, the situation became unbearable. The rebels had solidified their control over most of the area, and it was clear that we couldn't stay any longer. My mother made the decision that we would leave, that we would try to make it to Monrovia, where there was still some semblance of government control. It was a risky move but staying in Gardnersville any longer would have been a death sentence.

We packed what little we had and set out on foot, joining a group of other families making the same desperate journey. The road to Monrovia was long and dangerous, filled with checkpoints manned by rebels who demanded bribes or worse. But we made it, against all odds. We reached Monrovia, where we hoped to find safety and maybe, just maybe, find my father.

Chapter 3

◆———❧———◆

First Encounter Tragedy

Till now, I shared with my readers what it was like to live in Liberia during the war. However, till now, I never got to experience the brunt of the war first hand. I have only heard about it or I was narrated to through our friends, neighbors, or peers. The rumors were heartbreakingly chilling, more so because everyone would hushed tones. I used to wonder what was like to actually go through the horrors or come face to face with those thugs who have no regard for human life.

So, the first time I heard gunshots in our vicinity, I was in complete shock. It felt like the world was shaking, shattering around the very boundary of my house. I felt the noise of it reverberating within me, shaking me to mt core. After all, I was just a kid who had always been shielded by his parents. Until that morning, I had been fortunate enough not to experience anything as sinister. It had been distant, so I always felt like it was happening in another world and no matter what happens my parents will keep me safe. It was a stuff for nightmare and had no place in the reality.

However, things change me for forever. The gunshots rang in our area, terrifying me to no end. It happened so close to our home that I felt like they would enter and put all those bullets in me. I was used to the silence of our neighborhood, but that day, those gunshots ripped through the silence we came to love, and suddenly, the horrors turned into reality. It was no longer just stories.

The fog lifted after what felt like an eternity. It may have only been a few minutes for the outside world but to me, it felt like an eternity. The reverie broke when my mother entered my room, calling my name. And just like that, I looked at her with fear in my eyes, like a toddler at his mother because he know she is the only anchor that can actually save her. I knew my mother would have answers, I knew she would protect me, I knew she would explain the situation and give me reassurance. I knew with her by my side, I'd survive and everything would be okay.

Even though it has been years now, I can still feel those gunshots reverberating through my very existence. It happened at the crack of dawn so I was fast asleep. As soon as the sound came, I was jolted awake. The sharp, deafening cracks were echoing through the streets. Now imagine a little kid who's jolted awake from his sleep, only to experience the horrors of the war. I felt like the air was sucked out of my lungs. I could feel my sanity leaving my body as the temperature around my room suddenly felt too hot to hear. The air around me was thickened with dread as suffocation engulfed me whole. My unconscious mind had put up an alert front so it could faintly register the distant shouts coming form outside my room. In reality, it was too stunned to function or react to those sounds.

While the chaos was reigning outside my room, my insides were glued to my spot. I could barely move, as if somebody had frozen me to my spot. I could feel the dread of chaos coursing through my veins. I could feel how terrible it must have been for people outside my room. But I had no movement in me. I was afraid to even breathe.

My terrified heart was breathing erratically yet I could not feel it in my chest. Fear had made me unresponsive to my feelings. The only thing I felt was the suspension of time, as if the outside world had paused to take a collective breath.

To my horror, her face was etched with fear. Till date I can never forget how terrified she looked, as if the life had been sucked out of her. Usually, she is a picture of calmness, always composed, ready to embrace anyone who would feel bad. But that day, her face was white with worry, and it suddenly felt like she had aged. Her eyes drooping with concern for the safety of her children. Just when I took a look at her face, I knew that was it; nothing would ever be the same.

When all of us got together, the fear got worse. The entire house seemed to hold its breath. We were afraid of even looking at each other. All we could do was wait, wait for it to either befall us or by some miracle, go away. My mother, in particular, had all her attention on the rebels. She was listening for any sign of what was happening outside or whether or not they will come to our house. It seemed like the minutes stretched endlessly. It might have been only a few minutes but each second felt like an eternity filled with the weight of uncertainty. We didn't know what was about to happen. We didn't know if it was the last time that we were together. We didn't know anything.

She wasn't there only to see the attackers, she was like a coiled cat ready to react if someone dared cross her path. I must say, she had put up an amazingly brave front but only I know how terrified she was. I could see her hands trembling slightly, betraying the brave exterior she was trying to maintain, and in that moment, I knew if someone comes inside, we are doomed.

It was a tense silence, punctured only by the muffled sounds of chaos outside. It felt like we had forgotten to even breathe. Even though I was scared to death, the fear on my younger siblings' faces broke my heart.

They didn't deserve it. They didn't deserve to be as fearful at such a young age. Forgetting everything, I ran toward them and hugged them close. They clung to me, their eyes wide with fear. There was an overwhelming urge bulling inside me to protect them, to shield them from whatever horrors awaited us.

Just as I closed my eyes and sent a silent prayer to the universe, a commotion erupted. It happened so suddenly that we didn't have the time to even react. A rush of voices surrounded us, and we could hear angry footsteps approaching us. Even though the footsteps were pounding on the ground, I could feel them pounding on my already terrified heart. To add to the chaos, a storm of gunfire erupted. None of us knew what to do or how to react to the sudden horror that has befallen us. However, my brave mother moved quickly, her instincts kicking in instantly. She waved at us in a dismissive manner and asked us to stay low.

All of us obliged without uttering a single word. She moved toward the window ever so slowly and peered out the window ever so cautiously. Even though I could feel her tensed posture, I'm sure no one from outside could see even the shadow of hers.

Luckily, nobody entered our house. However, I saw my mother getting paler by the second, as if she had seen a ghost. There have been rare moments when I saw her as pale as she was in that moment. After a while, she moved from the window slowly so no one could detect her, and came toward us. Without so much as a word, she brought us in the middle of the room, away from the entrance or any windows. Then, we found out why she resembled a ghost.

My mother took a deep breath in an attempt to compose herself for what she was about to say next. My heart was thumping in my chest because I knew we were about to come across a terrible piece of news. She told us that people were whispering outside the window that two of our fellow neighbors had been killed. No one knew who was responsible. They were unknown gunmen who could not be traced.

Those who have been killed had nothing to do with the government or with the rebels, at least not officially, not that we knew of. To make matters worse, their bodies were left in the open as a warning. It was a sign of trouble that our neighborhood was in.

The reality sank in even before we could make sense of this horror of information we just got. It was like a heavy weight that settled in the pit of my stomach. I thought I had been naïve, hoping against hope that these rebels would leave us alone because we haven't done anything or haven't been associated with any group. How stupid, right? They didn't care about anything. They had no regard for anyone or anything, a human being just a body to them that they could play and discard according to their whim. After all, those they killed were innocent civilians like us who got caught in the crossfire of a war that had nothing to do with them. They were killed randomly, senselessly, not to mention, terrifyingly. To those rebels, it didn't matter who they were. They just wanted to remind the rest of us that in a world torn by a stupid conflict, the line between safety and danger could very easily vanish in a moment, and that we had to brace ourselves for what was about to come for us.

Since it was the first time that I got a glimpse of violence, it has been etched in my memory. It's as vivid as something that happened yesterday. I can never forget how devastating it felt when I heard the gunshots and got to know about the killings in our area. To a young mind that hasn't even developed yet, it was a struggle to let it all in and process it all. I feared for my safety and the safety of my siblings who were even younger to have witnessed the horror we did. I still remember how frightened we were, huddled together in the that dimly lit room, how vulnerable we felt, how fragile our existence felt. All of it echoed through the walls of our house that we were now afraid to call home. have to find a way to go through the wreckage left in its wake. When we gave her puzzled looks, she said we'd have to move to a new place and leave this red zone. She didn't cry or mourn the loss of our neighbors. She didn't grieve their deaths, nor did she take a second to think about how their lives were snuffed out in an instant. Instead, she took matters into her own hands and decided to shield her family from the same fate, like the tigress she was.

It was a moment that transformed the innocence of my childhood an that of my siblings. it was a moment of acute awareness that darkness had engulfed us whole and there was very little that we could do to survive there. Because it was clear that the moment we step outside our doors, we'll be confronted with thugs and rebels who wouldn't think twice before stealing our lives.

Even though I was just a kid then, I had a profound understanding. Just as actors work according to their directors, I used to function according to my mother. If she was strong, I was strong; if she was weak, I was weak. And in that moment, it was the weakest I had ever seen my mother at. She was trembling with the thought of us confronting violence because it was clear that we weren't merely spectators to it now; it was now knocking at our door and we had no choice but to deal with it. The small cocoon of safety that we had built after leaving our home was about to be destroyed, and there was nothing we could do about it.

One thing that I deeply admired about my mother is that even in the face of adversity, she wasn't the one who would give up. She might feel stumped for a while, sure, but she would never back down or succumb herself to her fate. She believed in making your way on your own and that was what she taught us. So, even though the world we knew was crumbling, she said we would

We all knew in our heart of hearts that she was right. We needed to get to safety, and we needed to get there fast. There was no time to waste or ponder; we had to make quick decisions. Because staying in our home, even for another day, was no longer an option. The violence was closing in, and soon it would be us they would be hunting. So, we didn't waste any time, not even to prepare. Mom moved like a whirlwind, gathering a few essentials like food, water, a few clothes, and blankets. All this time while she was packing, she didn't say anything, not even a single word. We couldn't say anything either; all we knew was that we had to go, and we had to go now.

Since we didn't plan anything, we didn't have a destination in mind. So, the nearest town was the safest bet for us at the time. We didn't know how we would be welcomed there as every town was on target. Plus, it was a small place that didn't host many people. The good point was that it was quite near, a short distance from our home so we could move there quickly without having to take a long journey that would last us days. However, we were still skeptical. The journey was still intense, and I could feel like my heart was in my throat. I was worried about the consequences. What if we come across looters? What if the rebels stop us? What if the town wasn't as welcoming or accommodating as we were hoping it would? It seemed like the danger was lurking behind every corner.

Thankfully, nothing of the sort happened to us. We arrived there safely only to see that a lot of people from our town. We were a bit taken aback because we thought it was a small town with barely any people there. But to our shock, it was filled with people fleeing the violence. Many like us were scared for their lives and decided to leave their homes, just like us. They look exhausted, afraid, and desperate beyond measure. There was nothing that any of us could say or do that would have made us feel better.

However, even in the midst of it all, we managed to find a hint of safety there. It was somehow safer than where we lived. Without panicking about the flood of people, my mother took us all and found a small place for us to live. It was a cramped room that could not host us all. It barely had any space for us to even lie down. However, none of us dared to complain because it was a roof over our heads and we were safe there, and even for a brief moment, it felt like we could breathe again.

It was no like we were the safest there though. The violence was still close, closer than we initially thought. But we started to settle there. We worked hard to find food and water and to our delight, we were successful in securing the necessities of life. Every day, we would rejoice at the sight of food, no matter how basic it was. It felt like a small victory in a world that had suddenly become so hostile, so cruel.

Even though we tried to be as normal as we could, the lurking danger never let the fear leave us. Every sudden movement and very distant noise seemed to rattle us. Every time the wind blew or a twig was snapped outside, we would tense up as if the rebels would enter and kill us on the spot. I couldn't help but think worse about every little thing. That was no way to live; no one deserved to live in constant fear, but we couldn't do anything, we had to survive.

Just when we thought things were settling down, they took a turn for the worse. We saw many people came in from our old town, bringing with them a grim news. They informed us that the violence has gotten worse. The rebels were frequently killing people without any reason and are blatantly bold in their pursuit. Anyone they would come across, they'll torture for days, only to kill them in the end. No matter what you say or where you belong to, once they got the hold of you, they'd kill you mercilessly. And to make matters worse, their terror was escalating at an alarming rate and they were planning to switch towns.

This piece of news came as a shock to us. It wasn't safe anymore, like we thought. There were no victories to be celebrated and no one to turn to there. the increased violence was about to take hold of our new town.

The gunmen were about to wreak havoc over our place of safety and they were expanding their reach at an alarming rate. It was confirmed now that we were barely safe there. It was only a matter of time before they found us and most probably kill us.

Without thinking twice I looked at my mother and knew instantly what she was thinking. And with a straight face, she said that we would be moving again. None of us argued, knowing she was right. She was very clear in her orders that we would have to move to a far away place called Marry Camp. It was located in the Guthrie Rubber Plantation in Bomi County. The good thing was that it was far enough from the hold of the rebels. So, Mom thought it might offer us a semblance of protection, at least for a while. I sent a silent thank you to the universe for such a resilient mother whose instincts were so on point. I felt like it was the only place where we could disappear and wait for the violence to pass.

We had no time to prepare so we had to travel by a pickup truck. It was one of the most uncomfortable journeys of my life. The roads were rough, treacherous even. There were numerous checkpoints and patrols that kept stopping us on the way. But we had no choice but to wait. Every time someone would stop us, my heart would jump up, beating erratically. Every time, I could feel the air around me filling with dread. The journey felt uncomfortably unknown, something the child in me wasn't prepared for.

He beckoned his fellow soldier who was rifling through our belongings. He didn't care if the food and drinks were getting wasted. He treated them as if they were worthless. moments when I thought we wouldn't make it, when the truck struggled to navigate the rough terrain, and the fear of being stranded in the middle of nowhere gripped us all. But we pressed on, driven by the desperate need to escape the violence that had consumed our home.

Let me tell you about my first checkpoint. When the soldiers, who were supposed to be the protectors of civilians, waved at our driver, asking him to stop the truck, we all got out scared. They ordered everyone to get down and empty their pockets on the pretext of checking if we had anything that went against state laws. They were rough, surrounding us like vultures. They scanned us like we were machines, not caring about the sanctity of our humanity. All they wanted was to take the little we had left. We had no regard for what would happen to us as they were ready with their stupid justifications.

Even the little kid in me could see the greed in their eyes, hungry for anything that might benefit them. The way their hands lingered on their rifles creeped the life out of me. I could see their fingers twitching as if they were waiting for an excuse to use them.

"Where are you going?" one of the soldiers demanded, his voice cold and hard. I got so scared when he addressed us that I hid behind my mother's stoic figure. She was as composed as ever. Even if she was scared, she didn't show it. Very confidently, she explained that we were on our way to Marry Camp to get to safety. Even though my mother was clear and respectful, the soldier was least interested in her explanations. He had his eye on something else.

I could feel my heart pounding in my chest because I felt like something terrible would happen. Every second we spent there fueled my fear. Before I could realize, my fear was turned into anger. Even though I was a kid, the way they were treating food angered me to no end. Besides, they were critical of my mother, who meant the world to me even during the horrors of the war. Everything that I held at that time, every chance of survival I had, was being held hostage. They were treating it like trash, as if it meant nothing. So, I ideally my anger was through the roof.

After what felt like an eternity, the soldiers allowed us to leave, having found nothing of value or purpose. However, they took some supplies as "payment" for letting them pass. They ad no shame, no regards for any of us. Even though there were plenty of children in our truck, they didn't pay heed to any of us. Imagine how heartless they were. It felt like a violation when they pushed us and asked us to leave. It felt as if we had been stripped of our dignity. These were the people who were supposed to protect us, to keep us safe from the violence tearing our country apart. But instead, they were part of the problem, exploiting the chaos for their own gain.

As we continued on our journey, the landscape around us became more desolate, the roads more dangerous. There were another checkpoint, we encountered a different group of soldiers. These men were even more hostile, their eyes dark with suspicion as they questioned us. They accused my mother of lying, of hiding something from them. I could see the fear in her eyes as they surrounded her, their hands resting on their weapons, ready to strike at any moment.

For a brief, terrifying moment, I thought they were going to kill her. The tension was palpable, and I could feel my body shaking with fear. But somehow, my mother managed to calm them down, convincing them that we were just a family trying to survive. It was a miracle that they let us go, but the experience shook me to my core.

By the time we finally reached Marry Camp, we were exhausted, both physically and emotionally. The journey had taken its toll, and the fear of what we had left behind still lingered in the back of my mind. But for the first time in days, there was a sense of relief. We had made it, and for the moment, we were safe.

Marry Camp was not what I had expected. It was a temporary refuge, filled with others who had fled the violence, just like us. There was a sense of camaraderie among the people there, a shared understanding of what we had all been through. But even in this place, far from the gunfire and the chaos, there was no escaping the fear. We were all waiting for the next attack, the next wave of violence that would send us running again.

The political situation in Liberia had become a nightmare. The country was tearing itself apart, and there seemed to be no end in sight. Charles Taylor's rebels were gaining ground, fueled by a deep-seated desire to overthrow the government and take control of the country. But the violence wasn't just about politics it was about power, revenge, and the deep tribal divisions that had festered for years.

The government, under Samuel Doe, was crumbling, unable to maintain control as the rebels advanced. Doe's regime had been marked by corruption and brutality, and many people saw the war as a way to rid the country of his oppressive rule. But in the process, innocent lives were being destroyed, families torn apart by the violence. The rebels claimed to be fighting for liberation, but their methods were just as cruel and indiscriminate as the government they sought to overthrow.

In the midst of it all, we were just trying to survive. We had no part in the politics, no stake in the power struggles that were tearing our country apart. But the war didn't care about that. It didn't care about who was innocent or who was guilty. All it cared about was destruction.

Marry Camp wasn't a permanent solution it was just a temporary stop on a much longer journey. But for now, it was enough. We had found safety, and in a world that had become so dangerous, that was all we could ask for. As we settled into life at the camp, I couldn't shake the memories of the journey. The fear, the violence, the feeling of helplessness it all stayed with me, a constant reminder of how close we had come to losing everything. The world outside Marry Camp was still burning, and I knew that sooner or later, we would have to face it again. But for now, we had found a moment of peace, however fragile it might be. And in that moment, we learned to cherish each day as it came, because in Liberia, you never knew when the gunshots would come again.

Chapter 4

Entry to the Tribalism

I have always had to bear the consequences of having Kamara as my surname. However, things got truly worse when Bomi Hills came into the picture. It was the place where I had to confront the weight of my last name the most. By that time, things had gotten much worse. The tribalism had swept through our country like a storm, and it seemed like there was nothing that could be done about it.

For me and my family, Bomi Hills wasn't just another city that we were passing through. We didn't spend a fleeting moment there. We had no plans to take a detour either. It was a place where we planned to live and, consequently stay safe. At that time, we were only concerned about the safety of our family. We didn't want to be just another fatality that nobody cared about name could mean the difference between life and death. This was the reality that everyone had to deal with. Even though my family and I were skeptical and were struggling to grapple with it every day, we had to do what was required to make ends meet.

However, the thing about Bomi Hills was your identity was the basis of your survival. We knew that, yet we chose to stay there because we had no choice. At the time, it seemed like the only safe where we could take refuge. So, we decided to take a risk and move.

There, our identity became more than just a personal or family matter. Our surname wasn't just a word we could put after our name. It became a hassle. It became a question of survival. In a country torn apart by tribal divisions, having it wrong.

Sending a silent prayer, we arrived in Bomi Hills after what felt like one of the most harrowing journeys of our lives. We felt humiliated like never before. However, we had no choice and no one to complain to. All we knew was that we had experienced enough danger that we could deal with anything now. It was a do-or-die situation for us, and there was no way back. On top of that, a mere mention of our name could land us in trouble; in fact, it could get us killed.

To my young mind, it didn't make sense. How could a word be a looming danger to us, I'd often wonder? Then I got to know that it wasn't just a word or a name like others. It represented a tribe, the Mandingo Tribe, that was being targeted by the rebels without an ounce of mercy. It was being persecuted for no crime, even executed without a fair trial, just because they weren't one of the rebels and did not support the atrocities happening in the country. It seemed like our only crime was our name and ethnicity. It was tribalism at its most brutal, and it was a terrifying reality to live with, shocking as it might have seemed.

My mother, ever so wise, was always quick to act in the face of adversity. So, when we arrived at Bomi Hills, the first thing she instructed us to do was change identities. Did I say "instructed?" No, she ordered us never to speak of "Kamara" again. Even though we were just kids, all of us took the news with a certain level of maturity that might not have been expected from kids our age. She told us we had to obtain new identities if we wanted to live and that it was necessary to move quickly.

So, even before we could worry about our livelihood or food and necessities, we all started looking for ways to easily navigate this situation without being detected by the rebel authorities. Just as we were about to put our plan into action, we heard another grim news that the government forces and rebel groups were both scrutinizing people's identities, looking for any excuse to separate those they saw as "the enemy" from the rest of the population. It became "official" too soon. We heard Mandingos were being hunted, blamed for supporting the official government, even though many of us were just trying to survive like everyone else. The danger of being identified as Mandingo was all too real.

As soon as we got that news, it reminded me of the time when my father warned us about the repercussions of having Kamara at the end of our official documents. Then, we kids didn't think that it was as sire; however, now, things had taken the worst turn, and our hands were tied. At that moment, I was reminded of the sacrifice my father made for the safety of his family. He was left behind. He stayed back. He didn't get to see his family just because he didn't want us to come under the radar of these rebels. What was the point of all that? We were in danger anyway now, and I terribly missed my father. I so wished for him to be with us, but alas! His connection with the government, coupled with his Mandingo heritage, made it impossible for him to join us.

Now that we had been hearing stories of entire families being executed simply because of their tribal affiliation, we were silently thankful that Father didn't accompany us. The brutality was so no its peak that everyone, men, women, and children, were being killed for something they couldn't control: their name, their tribe, their identity. How stupid does that sound right now? But then, it was the reality of our lives, and we had to live with it anyway.

Keeping my feelings for Father aside, I accompanied my mother to get new identities. Let me tell you, it was a grueling process, even more grueling than moving to Bomi Hills. First of all, it was extremely dangerous for us to even attempt it. Secondly, what if we would get caught? There were so many complications associated with the mere thought of attempting this process.

However, my ever-so-pragmatist mother urged us all to take the chance, citing that it was the only mode of survival that we were left with. Otherwise, even if we survived Bomi Hills, the sinister aspect associated with Kamara would chase us till the end of our existence. We understood the gravity of the situation and vowed to be as helpful as we could to get through this exhausting process fractured by war, and now, on top of that, the looming danger of tribalism was hindering our process. Everywhere I went, we were met with suspicion. Everyone I met with made us feel like a culprit. Every now and then, we were afraid that they'd take us hostage and charge us with deception – the entire process was so nerve-wracking.

If we thought the process would be hard, it was an understatement. It was excruciatingly hard, something that jolted us to our very core. It seemed that nothing was working out for us. The arduous nature of the work was taking a toll on our already scared, tired hearts. And you know what the worst part was? We weren't even sure whether the efforts we were putting in would be fruitful or not. The uncertainty that came with it was like a dagger to our chests, killing us ever-so-slowly every day. During the initial part of the process, everything seemed bleak, and nothing seemed to have worked out for us.

In a war-stricken area, it's anyway a problematic task to do anything official. As for Liberia, things were even worse than other countries that might have been going through war. Since tribalism was wreaking havoc across the country, even the smallest tasks were taking an eternity to reach completion. It didn't feel like we were in our own country, requesting to change our own documents; it felt like we were captured under the reigns of tyrants and desperately looking for a way out, which was, of course, the truest, most straightforward explanation I can come up with now. The most time-consuming aspect of the process was going through the bureaucratic details. We were already.

And you can say that our anxiety levels were at an all time high because, in a way, we were doing something deceptive. We were giving up our identities, albeit to save our necks, but it was wrong nonetheless. So, we were always feeling guilty, our nerves getting the best of us. Every corner we turned, we thought we'd be captured and put to death. Since we had to lie about who we were, which tribe we belonged to, and which part of the country we came from, we couldn't afford to make any mistakes.

When we decided to start the process properly and arrived at the local government office in Bomi Hills, I was dangerously nervous. I still remember the tense atmosphere there, the place bustling with numerous officials peering at us curiously. We were asked to sit in the waiting room until the officer who would process our IDs came. It may seem like nothing, but to us, it felt like an inspection. At any moment, someone would come bustling through the door and strip us of the dignity we were left with.

Thankfully, we weren't alone there. The room was filled with people like us, all wanting to change their living conditions, all trying to escape the violence once and for all, all hoping to hide their true identities so they could live in peace. Even though I wasn't as old, I could see the fear in their eyes. I could understand their trepidation. I could feel the tension coming out of them.

In fact, it wouldn't be wrong to say that it hung in the air like a thick fog. Everywhere you looked, you could see dread reigning. Everyone your eyes meet seemed extremely cautious. All of us were careful beyond measure. We watched our words carefully and only said what was needed. We were so full of nerves that we even avoided eye contact with the officials. Why would we do that? They were the ones who could decide our fate with a single glance.

As we waited, I was sending silent prayers to the universe to protect us and make the process as smooth as possible. I had to leave my prayers abruptly when our names were called out. We were on our feet within seconds. We didn't have the time to collect ourselves because we were rushed into a small office almost instantly. All this while, I had this overwhelming feeling of guilt brimming in my heart. Why, you ask? To this day, I couldn't figure out the reason. It was just a strange feeling as if we were doing something wrong as if we were running after a train we were about to miss. As soon as we entered the small, dingy room, I pushed my thoughts aside and attempted to collect myself. I knew that we couldn't afford to stray out of line, so I tried to appear as calm as I could.

The officer we met with was stern, curt, and dismissive. He was sitting behind a wooden desk piled up with numerous papers and filed documents. Everything was in disarray, as if he didn't care enough about anything, neither about us nor about his job. He glanced at us briefly before motioning for us to sit down, and then something happened that made my heart beat erratically: the interrogation. Without wasting a second, he started asking us seemingly benign questions that felt like bulldozers to my scared little heart. At that moment, I realized that the untidy table and the scattered documents were the least of my worries.

"What is your name?" was the first question he asked. We answered almost robotically. Another question came, "Where are you from?" Another robotic answer. Then, the next question and most important question came, "What tribe do you belong to?"

When he asked us this question, his eyes narrowed as if he knew us from Adam. For a moment, I felt like he could see through my soul. He could see that we were about to lie. He could see us struggling to breathe.

Every word he uttered and every answer we gave seemed scripted. Every question he asked us felt like a potential trap we'd be trapped into. We knew that ifwe answered wrong and hesitated for even a moment, it could raise suspicions.

I am immensely thankful to my mother for shielding us from every step of the way. That interrogating session was no exception. She didn't let us talk too much. She tried to shoulder the burden of answering their horrific questions to the best of her abilities. To the outside world, she must have seemed like a calm and composed person, as if every word that escaped her lips was nothing but the truth. Her answers were so precise that it felt like she had been practicing the lies a hundred times a day. Her entire being radiated nothing but confidence. There were no signs of agitation; she composed herself well.

To this day, I don't understand how she did it all. She chose different names for all of us and uttered them with such confidence that even I believed those were our real names. She even concocted an imaginary story about our family, where we came from, what we did, and how we came to be. She told him that we belonged to a small village far enough from the place of conflict, even farther than the place where Mandingos were being hunted. I was so impressed with her conviction; it seemed believable even to somebody who knew us.

However, as impressed as I was, something didn't feel right. Something didn't sit well with me. Something felt off, as if it really was deceitful, as if we were really doing something wrong. And it was, wasn't it? To deny who we were, to be ashamed of our identity, to hide our identity. My heart kept urging me to give it all up, but my head knew my mother was doing the right thing. My head knew it was essential to fool the officer, to make him believe that we had nothing to do with the tribe they hated. My head knew survival was all that mattered. It was the need of the hour, now more than ever.

When my mother was done, the officer looked up and peered into my mother's skin as if he wanted to see through her, as if he wanted to verify the answers. I had to give it to him, and he was attentive throughout the session and listened carefully to what we had to say. He kept looking up from the papers in front of him to assess my mother's answers. All this while, our nerves were tingling as if, at any given moment, we would be busted.

After what felt like hours of questioning, he finally nodded and motioned for us to leave. We had passed the test. I couldn't believe it! WE HAD PASSED THE TEST IN THE FIRST GO! I couldn't believe our luck. It felt like an incredible win. He told us that we would receive our new IDs in a few days and we wouldn't have to come down to the office again. Even though I was incredibly happy that the hard part was over, the weight of what we had done, of what we had been forced to do, settled heavily on my heart, but no matter what I felt, we couldn't go back. It was done and dusted.

If I tell you the truth, the happiness I felt was only fleeting. For a second, I thought the hard part was truly over. However, the days waiting for the new ID were the real test of our patience, not to mention the anxiety that came with it.

We had seen many people being dragged out of their houses into the streets because they were caught faking their identities. The paperwork went through, and the results came out, declaring them fake. Numerous families in our neighborhood were dragged and publically shamed, some of them even mutilated and killed for their treachery. So, every time I heard a knock at the door or saw a soldier pass by, I felt a surge of panic rising in my chest. Would they come to know the truth? Would they discover who we really were? Would they drag us out into the streets like they had done to so many others? And worst of all, would they kill us? The uncertainty was maddening.

Days went by in fear. One day, I awoke in my bed, dreading the wailing noises that had become the norm. I sent a silent prayer to the universe to let us have our IDs today so we could relax a bit. To my absolute delight, we finally received our new IDs the very same day. There was a small sense of relief, a feeling that felt foreign after continuously feeling the absolute worst all the time, for all these days. Whatever it was, we knew that, at least for now, we could get the obnoxious rebels off our backs. For a little while, we had some semblance of protection. For the time being, the curse that followed the name "Kamara" had been lifted.

Now, it was time for action. We had to move again and move fast. Even though we were free of the tribe name, a new load burdened our shoulders: the burden of living a lie. No matter how much we think we succeeded in concealing our identities, our hearts knew the truth. Our entire existence was laced with lies, but there was nothing we could do about it. Keeping all these thoughts aside, we left Bomi Hills, hoping to find refuge and solace in a new place. My mom decided to choose Marry Camp, located in the Guthrie Rubber Plantation in Bomi County. During the entire journey, we were scared by the idea of investigation. Even though we had our new IDs with us, the fear persisted: what if they found out our reality?

Thankfully, none of that happened. We reached there without any trouble or unnecessary hindrance from the rebels. However, as soon as we stepped there, there was a certain emptiness in the air, I could feel it in my bones. I could feel our hopes for a better life crushing. I couldn't quite put my finger on what it was that led me to think that it was just an eerie feeling that refused to leave me.

And I was right. Life was far from easy there. We had to live in camps that were filled with people like us who had nowhere to do, who wanted to flee from the places they were oppressed in, where they wanted to flee the violence. Tensions were high in our camps. Food and water were scarce, and the constant threat of rebel attacks loomed over us like a dark cloud. But the most difficult part of life at Marry Camp was the need to constantly hide who we were. We couldn't tell anyone our real name. We couldn't mention the fact that we were Mandingo. We had to live in a state of constant vigilance, always aware that one slip of the tongue could lead to our deaths.

The precautions we took to avoid revealing our true identity were extreme. We never spoke about our past, never mentioned our relatives or our hometown. Even within the confines of our small group of family and friends, we were careful. My mother was the most cautious of us all. She was so vehement that it felt like she was drilled into us. We had to keep our stories straight. We had to make it believable. We were never supposed to let our guard down.

If you ask me the truth, the constant fear, the constant vigilance, the constant lying was exhausting beyond measure. Living under that kind of pressure was bearable for every one of us, but it was necessary. We had seen what happened to people who were discovered to be Mandingo, and we didn't want to succumb to the same fate.

Sometimes, I wanted to chuckle at the irony of the situation we were in. We were in hiding, not because of anything we had done, but simply because of who we were. The fact that I was born into a Mandingo family and that I had a name that connected me to a particular tribe was enough to make me a direct target. Doesn't it sound absurd?

Especially today, when I think about it, it makes my blood boil, but during those terrible days, it was the reality of the war. Tribalism was turning neighbor against neighbor and friend against friend. Everyone was betraying in the hopes of saving their neck. People were being killed for the most random reasons, such as their last name, their accent, or where they were born.

The paranoia at Marry Camp was palpable. Everyone was afraid, not just of the rebels but of each other as well. You never knew who you could trust. People were constantly trying to figure out who belonged to which tribe, who was loyal to the government, and who was sympathetic to the rebels. It felt like a dangerous game to me, and the stakes were life and death.

I remember one incident in particular that shook me to my core. A man in the camp, someone we had seen around but didn't know well, was accused of being a Mandingo. His name had come up in conversation, and someone, whether out of malice or fear, I don't know, had reported him to the camp authorities. They dragged him out of his tent in the middle of the night. They were so brutal that they didn't care about anyone or anything. They didn't stop or think about this family. The only thing they were concerned about was his name. They dragged him into the street and beat him black and blue. After the terrible beating, they pulled him close and took him away. We never saw him again.

The thought that something like that could happen to us at any moment was terrifying. After all, we were all connected to Mandingo, the same as him. So, it was quite obvious that the mere mention of our name could land us in the same situation. Our existence didn't matter to the officials. They had no respect, no regard for anyone's life. All they cared about was being true to their agenda, no matter how many lives were lost. It didn't matter that we were just trying to survive, that we had no part in the political struggles tearing the country apart. In the eyes of the rebels, in the eyes of those who had given in to tribalism, we were guilty simply because of our identity.

Living in Marry Camp under these conditions took a toll on all of us. We were constantly on edge, never able to relax, never able to let our guard down. Even among our closest friends, there was always a sense of distance, a reluctance to share too much. We couldn't trust anyone, fearing that they might turn us in. It felt like trust had become a luxury we couldn't afford, like many other things.

As the days turned into weeks and the weeks into months, we realized that Marry Camp wasn't the safe haven we had hoped it would be. The gnawing feeling in my heart was getting stronger day by day. I didn't know why, but I could feel like our days there were numbered. It was a weird feeling enticed by the persistence of violence. I could feel the violence was closing in on us again.

We knew that it was only a matter of time before we would have to move once more. But where could we go? Where could we find a sanctuary? Where could we seek safety? The entire country seemed to be consumed by hatred, tribalism, and the kind of senseless violence that didn't care about who you were as a person. It only cared about the tribe you belonged to.

The burden of living under a false identity of constantly hiding who we were, weighed heavily on us all. But there was no alternative. To reveal the truth would be to invite death. So, we continued to lie, to live in the shadows, to cling to the hope that one day, this nightmare would end. But in Liberia, during those dark days of war, hope was a fragile thing. And the burden of a name, of an identity you couldn't change, was something we carried with us everywhere we went.

Chapter 5

Your Strength Begins in Tyranny

Marry Camp was a land of many trials for us. The day always begins before the sun had fully risen. I always felt that the usual glow of the sun had always been missing. Probably it was the effect of the ongoing war or a warning of the upcoming episode of tyranny we were about to deal with. Whatever it was, I felt, the sun always casted a muted glow over the ever-sobroken landscape of Marry Camp. There was a gloom in the air that never left us, melancholy reigning as if destined for us. Everywhere we looked, there was hopelessness, heartbreak, and sorrow.

It wouldn't be wrong to say that every morning carried a promise of chaos that could disrupt your life in the blink of an eye. We never knew what fresh hell we would wake up in that day. We never knew what awaited us. We had no idea when it would strike. All we knew was to be cautious, even of the shadows crossing by us.

I still remember some mornings that were eerily quiet. Those were the days that we were most scared of. There was certain silence in the air, silence that used to pierce through our horrified hearts. Any given moment, it could turn into a wail of tyranny, killing who knows who in its wake. Whenever we felt like it was quiet, too quiet for our liking, as if the world had been put on pause for the day, we would hold our breath, praying and chanting a few mantras we knew. After all, a known hell is way better than an unknown heaven, or so grief-stricken people would have you believe.

I think there is a certain calm in the known chaos, something that you are handling and navigating through every day would have you believe that you can do it all over it. Therefore, when chaotic mornings greeted us, we'd embrace ourselves and get ready to fight back without an ounce of a thought. We would wake up to the sharp sound of gunfire and the ground shaking blasts of RPGs tearing through the air, bringing with it an unbearable sense of dread, the kind of dread that terrified us to our very souls, the kind of dread that oddly seemed familiar.

During such moments, I could feel the air around me vibrating with danger. I could feel the imminent menace looming. I could feel my life slipping through my fingers. It didn't happen once or twice, it was routine for the resident of Liberia. The entire country was on fire, where people where losing themselves, their dignities, their lives, every other minute. Everyone had to live every second walking on eggshells, knowing one wrong move would land us in hell.

Let me tell you about this one incident. I was asleep, but not really. You know the kind of sleep where you have your yes shut but your subconscious is alert, ready to pounce at the slightest noise. I used to be a sound sleeper because this fiasco, sleeping and hugging my mother all night long. However, ever since we got displaced, sleep eluded me, making it challenging for me to sleep peacefully. Every night, it felt like I was sleeping with my eyes open, afraid that the moment I'd close my eyes, something terrible would happen to me or my family.

So, one morning, the crack of gunfire ripped through the early hours, jolting us awake. It was so early that even the sun wasn't out. The gunfire was so ferocious that we couldn't ever address each other over the noise of it. Then, something worse followed: the explosions of RPGs. Everyone scattered around shifted their place. We were all huddled around my mom, who was scared beyond measure. She was hugging us close, sweat trickling down her face as if she had run a marathon.

The explosions shattered whatever calm we had managed to salvage from the previous night. The relentless noise filled the air, and fear gripped us all before we even had time to understand what was happening. We had no idea what was unfolding outside our camp, or what was the cause of the sudden ruckus. All we knew was that we had to protect ourselves from the rebels. The situation was dire, and we were at our worst, feeling helpless, waiting for a miracle.

Do miracles really happen? Will someone come and save us from this tyranny? Is there a place where we could breathe freely? I had all these questions running through my mind. My heart, on the other hand, raced rapidly, pounding in my chest as I glanced at my family, each one of them frozen in terror. I had this terrible fear in my heart that this could be the last time that I was seeing them. We all knew what was coming next. What knew what happens next. The rebels had arrived again, and whenever they did, they brought with them brutality and killings. They ripped apart families, humiliated women, and orphaned children without an ounce of remorse. Their brutal reign of control and violence was bane of our existence.

Was there an end to it? No. Not in that moment, at least. It seemed like it was our fate to be terrified of these rebels all the time. It seemed like the universe had written contempt for us. It seemed like our lives were succumbed to a puddle of worthlessness, where no one cared if we lived or died. We were like peasants anyone could walk all over.

Living in Marry Camp was everything that morning entailed: terrifying chaos. It meant living in constant fear of these rebels who had made life a living hell. They were perpetrators of ferocity and vehemence when they were supposed to be our protectors, shielding us form the atrocities of war. They were supposed to keep us sane, not drive us insane. They were supposed to provide us with means for sustenance, not snatch our will to live.

I wanted to almost laugh at the irony of the situation. When the war started, we were told that rebels were in our favor and they would be fighting for the liberation of the common men from the horrors of tyranny.

Instead, they turned into tyrants always killing people. All they had done was turn the camp into a prison. We used to feel like our camps were a place where death was always lurking around the corner. They terrified us to no end. Every day was a test of survival in their presence. Every day we had to remind ourselves to stay invisible, to keep our heads down, to blend in.

I had never felt so small in my life, like an ant scurrying around, hoping not to get crushed. I had always been a curious child, always trying to learn new things, always wanting to know more. But ever since the war started, I felt I had been shut down, shunned in the corner. This is because knowing too much or asking too many questions can be life-threatening. Still, my young mind always wondered what went wrong in those rebels' head that they had to be so horrific to innocent people. How could they not feel anything? How could they not have any regard for anyone? How could they convince themselves to snatch the life out of an innocent soul? These questions baffled me to no end.

I've always had an inquisitive nature that pushed me to the edge. Even that day, even though we were terrified beyond measure, curiosity piqued inside me, urging me to wonder what was happening outside. We could hear the constant firing, but we had no clue why. What was so important so early in the morning that they had to wreak havoc over our camp at such an early hour?

So, while my family was right in the middle of the room, clinging to my mother, I found myself edging towards the small hole in the window side of our makeshift home. I'd call it home because it had been protecting us from the horrors, no matter how small or dingy it was. Even though I had been scared in those premises, there was a certain sense of calm that engulfed me there. In that moment, I was unbelievably terrified, but the fear that had paralyzed me was suddenly overcome by an intense need to know.

Thus, without thinking twice, I let my inquisitive nature win and decided to see what lay out there. When I pressed my face against the cold wall and peeped through the hole, squinting my eyes, I saw something that got imprinted on my mind, something I still cannot forget, no matter how hard I try. It had a haunting effect on my mind.

There were heavily armed men, dropping from trees like insects, their shadows creating a horrifying scene all around our camp. It felt like the skies were spewing them out, unable to keep them in. All those men had their rifles out, which were gleaming in the dim light. Since the sun wasn't out properly, the scene was properly lit. the dimness of the day made the scene even more intriguingly terrifying.

I could almost swear that those men were extremely precise in their movement, their precision almost petrifying, as if they had rehearsed this scene a thousand times, as if they knew exactly how they wanted to act, as if the entire reason of their existence is to perform this scene that was unfolding before me at an unusual hour.

The thing that most disturbed me was how hard their faces were. There was no shadow of feeling, no reaction, nothing. There just had a robotic expression that felt like it had been plastered on their faces. When they spoke, you would feel that they word were coming out an animal, unfeeling, barking orders in harsh voices. There was nothing humane about their demeanor. I still remember their words, "Everyone, out now! Hands up, or you will be shot!"

There was something so sinister about their words. They were threatening us, as usual, but there was something different that day, something worse, something so menacing. The command was final, absolute. There was no room for disobedience. Not that anyone would ever dare to contradict them or stand in front of them or deny their orders. Everyone knew what happens if you dare to defy them.

Since I was the one seeing this scene unfolding right before my eyes, I felt the most brunt of it. My breath caught in my throat. The disturbing scene was too much for my already frightened, young heart. My curiosity had pushed me to the edge once again, a place from where I could never come back. Every time I was blinking, I could see a man dropping like fireflies. So, without wasting another second, I pulled away from the hole, wishingfor it to go away, hoping against hopes that when I'd get back to my mother, all of it would be over. Fear wrapped its icy fingers around my chest and I knew, in that moment, that it would forever be imprinted in my mind.

When I got back to my mother, wanting to be away from that hole, as far away as possible, something snapped inside me. I realized that It was in moments like this that survival instinct kicked in. There was no room for hesitation. No matter how many times you think it was it, there was no way you wouldn't fight back when push comes to shove. You would move; you had to move to save your neck. You woul have to act quickly to save yourself and your family no matter what the situation was. You had to think quickly, or you wouldn't make it. You had to think quickly, too. You'd have to push your brain to concoct a new idea then and there, even if you feel like it starts buffering under pressure.

While I was preparing myself, trying to train my mind, my mother quickly took charge of the situation. She was on her feet before anyone could ever move a muscle. She grabbed my hand and pulled me close to her, searching my face for something, anything. I didn't know what she wanted to see. Probably she wanted to see if I'd been traumatized by the scene in front of me or probably she was trying to look for signs of distress that would stop me from following her was nothing tying us to the government. There was nothing that I gave any evidence against us. But were they concerned about anything? Did they even care about any evidence? Were they even trying to be fair? The obvious answer was no.

When I looked back at her, I saw the terror in her eyes, but I also saw something else strength. She had bloodshot eyes, perhaps from crying out of fear. But there was determination, a will to protect her family, a will to never back down. She had this incredible ability to find courage in the darkest hours, and I truly believed it was that courage that kept us all together, no matter what the circumstances were.

Her grip on my hand hardened when she found what she was looking for on my face. To date, I couldn't quite put my finger on it; however, I could only deduce that she wanted to see what I would do if she decided to leave the camp. She must have seen that even though I was traumatized, I would follow her to the ends of the earth. So, without saying anything, she left my hand, only to grab it again. The only difference was that now, she had all of us in her embrace. Her grip was firm as she led us outside, where the rebels were. They were already lining people up for interrogation.

When we reached the door, Mother left our hands. Once again, we were on our feet, ready to face the rebels. My siblings and I followed her in silence, our hands raised in the air just like everyone else. In that moment, I felt like a culprit, like I have committed a crime, waiting to be punished. And what was our crime? Existing.

Now that we had changed our identities, they had no regard whatsoever for anything, and they had taken full control of the camp by the time we went out. They behaved as if they were our rulers, reigning over us, owning us, and as infuriating as it was to a self respecting person, it was the truth we had to deal with. They were the rules of this small world where we were trapped. They exerted their power over us as if we they were theirs to rule over, as if they owned our very existence. It seemed like they were in control of the steps we took and the breaths we breathed.

The only way they could exert their power over us was through violence and fear. They dictated every aspect of our lives, when we were supposed to eat, when we could sleep, where we could go. We had to step out of our houses with their permission. Everything was upside down. But that morning, it was something else. It wasn't about control. It wasn't about regulating anything. It wasn't about governing our moves; it was something far more ominous, far more menacing. It was about life or death.

When we stepped out of the door, we knew all this; we realized how grave the situation was. So, we all vowed to be extremely careful with our answers. They began questioning us, but before that, they divided us in groups. We were being interrogated not as individuals, but as members of specific tribes. Everyone had a questionable look on their faces. They were as scared as we were, but everyone held their grounds, putting up a brave face.

"Which tribe are you from?" The rebel in charge asked the question over and over again, moving from person to person. I used to feel that this question was the crux of our existence; however, ever since we were displaced and had to live here, this one thing became the bane of our existence. We were continuously being dragged out just because of a certain tribe. The irony was even after changing our identities, we were scared to breathe the wrong word.

Moreover, the thing that most irked me was that they had a very cold, gruff way of dealing with the common people. Whenever they asked us anything, they behaved as if they wanted to spit in our faces. Even that day, the rebel who was questioning us had a cold, detached voice, as if he'd put us to death if we didn't say what he wanted us to say. I could feel the answer didn't matter much to him; he just wanted us to be terrified of us. He just wanted to control our emotions. He just wanted to keep us on edge. We all knew that the answers did matter to it, that if we didn't say the right thing, he'd have us killed then and there.

Every person who stood in front of him was given the same question, and the answer determined their fate. I could see it in his eyes, the way they darkened when someone said the wrong tribe, the way his lips curled into a cruel smile, as if he was taking pleasure in our misery, as if putting us to death was his ultimate fantasy. I felt sick to my stomach every time his eyes sparkled with the sinister glint.

We were all terrified of that moment the line of questioning that could expose who we really were. My family was Mandingo. Even though we had forged new identities, new names, there was always the fear that somehow, someone would discover the truth. My mother had drilled it into us repeatedly. She said, "Never say Kamara, never mention Mandingo, never tell anyone who you truly are." But when it was our turn, I could feel the terror rising inside each of us. We stood there, facing these men who had the power to end our lives with a single gesture, gearing up for the interrogation that was about to determine the course of our lives. They interrogated us and thankfully, none of us fumbled. We were confident in our answers.

Once the interrogation was done, the rebels began separating people by tribe, pulling certain people out of the line and pushing them toward the edge of the camp. There was no explanation, no reasoning. It was as if they were sorting through cattle, deciding which ones would live and which ones would die. The process went on for what felt like hours, days even. I stood there, watching as people were taken away, some of them sobbing, others too shocked to speak. The sound of gunfire echoed in the distance. It was a reminder of what awaited those who were chosen.

After the interrogation, some were allowed to return to their homes, trembling but alive. But others were not so lucky. Those who had been separated by tribe, those who were marked as "enemies" were led away, never to return. We knew what that meant. We all knew what their fate would be, even if we didn't speak it aloud. The rebels didn't need to explain. Death was the only outcome for those who belonged to the wrong tribe.

The horror of that morning was not an isolated incident. It became the rhythm of our lives at Marry Camp. Every day was a test, a gamble. We had to be careful with every word we said, every action we took. Even a casual conversation could betray us, could reveal the truth about who we were. My family lived in a constant state of fear, always watching our backs, always wondering if someone had noticed something, if someone would turn us in. It was exhausting, both mentally and physically.

The toll that this kind of living took on us was immense. My siblings and I, still children, struggled to understand why we were being hunted, why we had to hide who we were. But the adults, my mother especially, carried the weight of it more heavily. The constant fear, the sleepless nights, the knowledge that death was always close, it wore her down. I could see it in her eyes, the way her shoulders slumped, the way her once confident demeanor had been replaced with a quiet resignation.

The psychological impact of living under the control of the rebels was devastating. It wasn't just the physical danger that haunted us; it was the mental strain of never knowing when the next attack would come, when the next interrogation would begin first morning. The questioning was always the same, cold, methodical, and deadly. Each time, more people were taken away, and each time, the fear that we would be next grew stronger. We learned to read the signs, to understand the subtle cues that indicated who was in danger. But there was no escaping the fact that, in the end, our survival depended not on who we were as individuals, but on which tribe we belonged to.

For the children in the camp, the constant violence had a profound effect. Many of us became desensitized to the sound of gunfire, to the sight of blood. But at the same time, we carried an overwhelming sense of fear. Every night, I would lie awake, listening to the distant sounds of fighting, wondering if tomorrow would be the day the rebels came for us. The adults tried to shield us from the worst of it, but there was no escaping the reality of our situation. We knew what was happening. We knew that death was all around us.

As the days in Marry Camp dragged on, the rebels tightened their grip on the camp's residents. They demanded loyalty, but their loyalty was built on fear. They ruled through terror, controlling every aspect of our lives. We had no say in our future. We were at the mercy of men who saw us not as human beings, but as pawns in their war.

The process of isolating people by tribe became more frequent as the war progressed. Every few weeks, the rebels would round us up, lining us up in the same way they had that. And in the middle of it all, my family and I walked on eggshells every day, praying that we would not be discovered, praying that we would survive long enough to escape this nightmare.

Chapter 6

Marketing Strategy

No matter how hard we tried, the weight of survival bore heavily on all of us. Like I said, everyone had to walk on eggshells because one wrong move could have us killed. The interrogation that felt like the last exam was the norm now. Every time they'd come, we'd have a terrible feeling in our gut, as if it would be the last time we'd be seen breathing.

Things were so bad that finding food was a luxury. If you couldn't find your own food, you wouldn't be able to. The rebels, who claimed that they were in favor of the common men and their well – being, had no regard for those who wanted nothing but to go out of their houses to find sustenance for their families.

In my family, my aunt and sisters carried much of the burden of survival. They were the ones who didn't care about anyone or anything and ensured that we were all fed and tended to every day. Their determination led us to live a few days in peace without having to sleep on an empty stomach.

Needless to say, those were the most trying times of our lives. But the ladies of our house stepped up like no man could. They became the lifeblood of our small family, finding resources for us on a daily basis. Even when things became tough we didn't have any money, they procured essential goods for each one of us.

As the situation in the country got worse, food and supplies got scarce. The constant killings gave rise to more ammunition, with the government constantly spending on it. It eventually led to the fragility of the economy. Everything took a severe hit during the war. The government at the time was helpless and, obviously, could not protect anyone. The officials were nowhere to be seen, and nobody came to our aid.

Consequently, we had to fend for ourselves. Every morning, my aunt and sisters would steel themselves for the grueling task of going to the markets. These were not conventional markets; instead, they were like makeshift stalls that had been erected in camps and abandoned areas hastily. The war had destroyed the formal structures of society. It had left a landscape that offered nothing but chaos and desperation. Everyone was on the fence, but we had to make do. In the fractured world we were living in, more like barely surviving in, we were deprived of basic goods. Things like rice, palm oil, salt, and dried fish had become more precious than gold.

With the economy in free fall, the currency had lost its value. Even those who had money were nervous about the worsening situation of the country. In fact, money had been rendered nearly useless because there was no use for it. Since every one was scared of getting caught, those who had goods, even in a scarce quantity, wanted something in return they could use. They weren't interested in the money.

So, bartering became the only mode of survival. Everyone who had to get something would have to be skilled in it; otherwise, they had to return home empty-handed. I must say that it was a skill that required shrewdness and a deep understanding of human nature, something that didn't come naturally to me. My aunt, on the other hand, had the knack to negotiate fiercely. She knew what she had to do to make ends meet. She would always weigh the worth of her goods against the needs of the vendors and didn't back down easily. I always felt like every transaction was a delicate dance to her. Even though it was fraught with tension and uncertainty, she would be victorious almost every other time.

Families fought tirelessly to secure the basic necessities of life. Each day was a battle against scarcity as they sought out food, clean water, and essential supplies. With every visit to the market, they had to go through declining market conditions. It was a new challenge, one that was fraught with uncertainty. My aunt, whenever she returned home, would always tell us that the most ordinary items had become hard-won treasures.

I have personally seen everyone around me struggling so their kids wouldn't have to take the brunt of it. However, it broke my heart to see the urgency of their struggle; it was palpable how parents made difficult choices. I saw them weighing the needs of their children against their own, often sacrificing themselves so their little ones could survive somewhat comfortably. Did I say comfortably? Hah! Comfort was a foreign concept for the people of Liberia at that point.

So, we had to make do with the little we had. In the relentless fight for survival, every small win was important. Every small victory felt monumental. Every little thing that we could get our hands on reminded us that it could all go away in the blink of an eye. At the same time, it also served as a reminder of the resilience we all had in the face of overwhelming challenges.

But it wasn't as easy as said. Everyone could see that amidst the clamor of voices and the scent of spices that were mingling with the dust, every other person who had even little means was mirroring the soul of a tyrant in their own way. There was an unspoken camaraderie among the market-goers, all united by their shared plight.

The markets were an unpredictable and dangerous place. The tension there was thick. It was a living entity that wrapped around every stall and alleyway. Soldiers and rebels, often high on power and perhaps substances, roamed the area like wolves on the prowl. We could actually see their eyes gleaming with a mix of suspicion and greed. They were scrutinizing every transaction with a predatory gaze, always ready to exert control and impose their will on anyone who had the audacity to step out of the line.

But I must say, I had immense respect for my aunt, who was a tough presence amidst this chaos. She was a strong woman with an iron will. Her quick thinking and sharp instincts became our salvation in this deceitful environment. Like I said, her words flew like water, soothing and persuasive. It was as if she could read the very thoughts of those around her, discerning their fears and desires with uncanny accuracy.

In the face of intimidation, she remained a pillar of calm. While others might falter, her resolve only hardened. She went through the shifting dynamics of the marketplace with grace, her sharp eyes scanning for danger while her mind raced with strategies. With every negotiation, she wielded her knowledge like a weapon. She ensured our safety while cleverly securing the supplies we needed.

In a world where loyalty could shift like sand and danger lurked around every corner, my aunt was our anchor. She reminded us that even in the darkest of places, there was strength to be found in clarity of purpose and the courage to stand firm. Each day in the market was a test, but with her by my side, I learned that survival was not just about strength; it was about intelligence, intuition, and the bond of family.

You know what really amazes me? How little, seemingly insignificant things become so important during times of need. The same thing happened during the war in Liberia. Would you believe it if I told you that salt became the most important entity there could be? Yes, you read that right. People were fighting to procure a packet of salt almost every other day. Even those with money were searching desperately for it, but to no avail. Those who had it were preserving it, only letting it out if they were offered something way more valuable. If you ask me the truth, during those times, there was nothing more important than food, not even gold.

Since things were getting worse, there had to be someone who knew the language of those markets, someone who had the knack to barter, someone who didn't get afraid of the politics that had been going on. Thankfully, we had our aunt. To make things a little better, she would take my sisters along so that they could learn the art of bartering, too.

Initially, my sisters were intimated with the idea of going into the market and facing those rebels. However, my aunt calmed them down. She reiterated the fact that if things go south, we all need to know how to make things happen for ourselves. Learning how to barter was the need of the hour, and everyone had to oblige if they wanted to survive.

So, my sisters went on a journey to fetch things for us almost every other day. However, it didn't take them long to see the unfair treatment of the market. Goods were exchanged unfairly, with vendors taking advantage of helpless people who just wanted to get food for their loved ones. Nobody had any choice but to listen to those vendors and do as they said.

My aunt trained my sisters to be adamant. She told them that if we were to survive this fraudulent market, we had to be cunning. We couldn't afford to be fair or have principles, accepting whatever we were given. We had to fight back and make things work for ourselves. She clearly mentioned that to provide even a small meal for our family, we had to be utmost resilient and firm in whatever we asked for. Even though the danger was looming all around, my aunt didn't back down. Instead, she remained focused and refused to let fear paralyze her. She didn't let anyone or anything get to herself; instead, she lifted our spirits too and showed us a way to get the food, especially my sisters.

According to my sisters, every trip to the market felt like walking on a tightrope over a pit of vipers, but my aunt never faltered. However, to them, the task was as daunting as walking into a lion's den. Even though they followed her into the heart of those markets, carrying whatever little we had, there was an air of uncertainty they could feel around them. All they hoped was to trade our little goods for something essential. But things weren't working out for them in the initial days of their market hunt. Sometimes, they would take a sack of rice with them; other times, they would take a small amount of Kerosene.

As they continued to accompany my aunt, they learned a thing or two about bartering. Every day, they would return home exhausted after a tiring day, but to our delight, they would have a little that could be sufficient for us. Sometimes, they would have a triumphant look on their faces when they returned, which meant they had managed to barter for just enough food to get us through a couple of days. We would also get happy, but deep down, we knew that the relief was temporary. The looming threat of violence, of things getting worse, hung over us like a shadow, and we were fully aware of that.

The violence and terror were rising by the day. It was getting more and more difficult for us to make ends meet. However, my aunt and sisters did not give up. They continued their daily hustle, caring about nothing but our well-being. However, it was even more challenging than before. Supplies became scarcer, so the bartering system became even more essential. They had an even bigger burden on their shoulders. Not only did they have to go through the dangers of the market, but they also had to be immensely careful of the schemes and violence of the rebels, who were now more active than ever. The threat was constant, but they had to make do.

So, every trip to the market became a calculated risk. They had to be careful not to ruffle any feathers or step on anybody's toes. There was no choice but to keep on going, no matter what the consequences would be. We all needed food and necessities if we wanted to survive, and there was no easy way to get it.

We struggled with the basic things like salt, matches, and cooking oil as things got worse. We never thought such things would become a luxury, but they did. I had seen people getting restless for a small amount of rice, willing to trade anything. They weren't thinking about the long run; they just wanted to get through one day at a time.

My sisters would often come and tell me that they felt helpless when they saw people crying and bartering their household items for a small amount of food. But they had no choice. Thankfully, they became experts at steering the market, spotting a good trade, and avoiding the eyes of suspicious soldiers. They knew how to make quick deals and how to tip the scales in their favor quietly. They knew they had to be smart about it; otherwise, we wouldn't be able to retain our dignity, and if worse came to worst, we would all be doomed.

Despite knowing their situation, they were constantly skeptical. No matter how well they did in the market or how many rations they would get for us, the constant fear of violence was ever-present. It overshadowed every move they made, every strategy they used, every vendor they won over. They knew that at any moment, without warning, the situation could escalate, and they could be captured. After all, they had seen people getting beaten and dragged away from the market for the smallest infractions. Naturally, they were scared. They were one step away from a disaster, and that knowledge weighed heavily on them every day.

The precarious balance we maintained was shattered when we started hearing rumors of another warring faction approaching. The camp was already under the control of one rebel group, and we had barely survived their tyranny. Now, a counter-attack was coming, and the violence would only escalate. War had a way of creating alliances and enemies overnight, and the shifting loyalties of the factions meant that no place was ever truly safe.

The news reached us in bits and pieces, whispered among the residents of the camp. There was fear in every voice, and with good reason. The faction that controlled our camp had brutally repressed any sign of resistance. We had seen people publicly executed for the smallest of infractions. Their bodies were left as grim warnings to others. If the new faction took control, it would be even worse. We knew they would come with a vengeance in their hearts, killing indiscriminately and leaving chaos in their wake.

It was this impending threat that spurred us into action. The market hustle could no longer sustain us; we needed to escape before it was too late. There was no question about it because staying in the camp meant certain death. We had heard stories of families who had stayed behind, trapped between factions. We had seen their lives snuffed out in the blink of an eye.

But escaping was easier said than done. The rebels had set up checkpoints around the camp to prevent anyone from leaving. The consequences for attempting to escape were severe. If you get caught, you would either be executed on the spot or dragged back to the camp, where you would be made an example. We had witnessed these punishments before. Families who had dared to leave were brought back. They were beaten and bloodied. We could see that their fates were sealed by the rebel leaders.

The sight of their suffering was heartbreaking and terrifying beyond measure, especially for us kids. They were mutilated, and some were even left to die. The constant struggle, the bloodied sights, and the horrible conditions were taking a toll on us. The escalating situation was unbearable and had left a permanent mark on all of us. It was a constant reminder of the high stakes, and it was time to take matters into our own hands by leaving.

We had made up our minds. We had to move at any cost. We had to make it by hook or by crook, but we had to be careful. We couldn't afford to let this news get out of our house. There was so much that was happening, so many things to factor in. Most importantly, we didn't know whom to trust. Everybody was scared, and they were doing everything they could to save their necks, even if it required betraying others.

So, we started planning slowly. Even though we were desperate, we didn't let it get to our heads. We started with careful calculations, making sure that everything was kept under wraps. My aunt, with her sharp mind and market connections, began to quietly gather information. She asked around, subtly probing people she trusted for details on the safest routes out of the camp. My sisters, too, were discreet, listening to rumors and whispers about other families who had successfully escaped. It was a delicate balance. We knew showing too much interest or asking too many questions could easily raise suspicion.

Now, it was a matter of when. We knew how heavily guarded the checkposts would be, so leaving during the daytime was out of the question. We decided that the only way to escape would be under the cover of night. Since there was darkness all around us, we could have a slim chance of slipping through unnoticed. It would surely be dangerous, but it was our only option. We planned to leave with nothing but the clothes on our backs and whatever small valuables we could carry, knowing that even the slightest sign of preparation could tip off the rebels.

As the day of our escape approached, the tension in the camp became unbearable. Every noise made me jump. Every glance from a soldier felt like a death sentence. My mother and aunt were the calmest of us all. They had a stoic presence, their faces devoid of any emotion. If I didn't know better, I'd also believe that it was any other day. However, since I was aware of the situation, I could see the strain in their eyes. They knew the risks, but they also knew that staying was not an option. And I could understand their dilemma. It wasn't just them; fear and determination waged war inside all of us.

Life under rebel control had been a daily struggle for survival. The rebels were ruthless and unpredictable, and any small mistake could result in punishment. We had learned to keep our heads down to avoid drawing attention to ourselves. But living like that, constantly on edge, took a toll on our mental health.

However, it was high time that we left it all behind. So, in the end, survival instincts took over. From the information that my aunt gathered, we found out a possible route out of the camp, one that led through a narrow forest trail that the rebels rarely patrolled. It was risky, but it was our best chance. We had to move quickly to avoid detection.

The night of our escape was tense. We gathered what little we had, knowing that we would need to travel light. My aunt led the way, her face set in determination. My mother, sisters, and I followed closely behind, trying to move as quietly as possible. The camp was eerily quiet. I could sense that the usual sounds of the market and the soldiers' voices were replaced by an oppressive silence.

As we made our way through the camp, my heart pounded in my chest. Every step felt like a potential misstep, and every sound like the approach of danger. But I took refuge in the warmth of my mother.

She remained calm, guiding us through the shadows with steady precision. The forest loomed ahead of us, dark and foreboding, but in my young mind, it represented freedom, as we would finally be free to breathe. I thought if we made it today, we could do whatever we wanted.

But my spirits were dampened the moment we stepped out of the camp. My heart was beating erratically, the weight of which I could feel in my throat. The journey was not without its challenges. The trail was treacherous, and it was filled with obstacles that slowed our progress. Since it was too dark, it was difficult for us to see. We stumbled over rocks and roots as we made our way through the forest. But we pushed on; we had no other choice. We knew that turning back was not an option.

The sounds of the camp faded behind us as we moved deeper into the forest. For the first time in months, I allowed myself to hope. We had made it this far. Perhaps we could truly escape the horrors of the war. Perhaps there was a way for us to leave it all behind. Perhaps there were good times on the horizon.

As dawn broke, we emerged from the forest, exhausted but alive. We had escaped the camp, but the world outside was still filled with uncertainty. The war raged on, and we would need to find a new place to call home. But for now, we had survived, and that was enough. The weight of survival had taken its toll on all of us, but we were stronger for it. We had carried each other through the darkest days, and I had hope that our resilience would eventually become our salvation.

Chapter 7

First Gruesome Thing

While we were crossing the forest amidst the chaos and uncertainty, something suddenly reminded me of the time when I had my first gruesome experience. It was so horrific that whenever I think about it, I get goosebumps. It was one of the most dreadful moments of my life, and I have been confronted with my fair share of such moments.

The wind was hot that day, thick with the humidity that clung to your skin and suffocated the air. But the physical discomfort was nothing compared to the emotional weight that seemed to bear down on all of us. It was a time when fear had become the air we breathed. Every morning began with the unspoken knowledge that the day could very well be your last. As usual, the political situation in Liberia had spiraled beyond the comprehension of any ordinary mind, and we were all over the place.

Now, I'm talking about the time back at Marry Camp. What started as a power struggle between corrupt leaders and factions had devolved into the most grotesque display of brutality imaginable.

There was no place for mercy, not even for children. There were no schools or activities for children because parents were afraid that their children wouldn't be safe out there. Things were surely chaotic, yet, in that chaos, there was something eerily normal about the horror.

You must be surprised, but no, I'm not kidding. I don't know if it was about the monotony or just the habit, but the chaos of the war became a part of life. It was a twisted version of normalcy. Initially, it felt like a new depressing thing that was wreaking havoc on our lives. However, as time passed, it became our new reality, a reality we wanted to escape but got habitual of.

One day, while the war was raging on, I got up, restless. That day began like any other– full of chaos. Yet, there was this unknown anxiety twisting in my chest. Like I said, to us, school was a distant memory that no one remembered. I liked the idea of going to school where I could escape reality, but of course, it was too dangerous to hold classes, and it had been a long, long time before I even thought about it.

I knew it was out of the question, yet I had an overwhelming feeling to leave the house and meet my friends, people who were the companions of my youth. You know that feeling you feel instantly at ease just because you have done something you liked with your friends? That was what I was craving. Joy was a foreign concept to us, yet the little hint of it only came to us siblings when we could spend a few hours with our friends. We knew that just like the war had ravaged the physical infrastructure, it had also ripped apart the social fabric of our lives. We understood the gravity of the situation, yet there was a yearning that only ceased to rest when we went out and spent time with our friends.

If you ask me personally, I often found comfort in swimming. Whenever it got too much or if I felt strangled, I always turned to the one true love I had water. There was something so serene, so beautiful about the flowing water that could not be found anywhere. Just when you look at it, you get to experience a feeling of peace washing all over you. But to step into it, to feel it sweeping across your skin, to let yourself go along its waves is an indescribable feeling. All I can say is that it takes you to another dimension, where there was no war, no chaos, no atrocities, a place where serenity takes over, and peace sneaks into your heart instantly.

So, during the hard days, I used to ask my friends to come over, and we'd go swimming. Luckily, there was a river not too far away from the camp. It was my absolute favorite place on the little earth that I had access to, a place where I'd have full control over my body, the only place where no other entity was controlling me or my moves.

For a little while, my body would cut through the water, and it would forget the ongoing violence it could have been subjected to any day.

Remembering this feeling, I decided to gather my friends again. So, I made my way through the winding paths of our war-torn settlement. I started knocking on doors, making sure not to attract unnecessary attention. I tried to call out my friends' names in hushed tones, hoping they would hear me and come out of their houses. To my dismay, none of my friends responded. A few of their parents came out and informed me again in a hushed voice that they weren't home. Others only waved at me, gesturing that the kids were out.

So, I figured they had already gone ahead to the river because it was a common meeting point for us. I didn't know what else to do or where else to go. Also, I had no idea what the time was. Ever since the war started, it eroded not just our freedom but also our sense of time. Nobody kept to a schedule anymore, and it felt like time was measured not in minutes or hours but in moments of survival. If you were lucky enough to spare a few hours to yourself without the constant monotony of gunshots, you'd find yourself lucky to go through another day.

That day was one of the rare occurrences in which I didn't feel commotion, which was why I decided to go after my friends on my own. If you ask me the truth, I was quite eager for the familiar coolness of the water. Otherwise, I would have returned home. But something came over me, and I decided to throw caution out the window and head towards the river. Little did I know that I was about to encounter something that would change my understanding of me forever.

Trying not to become too prominent, I edged towards the dirt road and started moving cautiously, the idea of gliding against the water occupying my mind. I wanted nothing more than just to go inside the river and let my anxiousness wash away. But that didn't mean that I turned a blind eye to the usual sounds of war echoing in the distance; I was very aware that things could go wrong at any moment, and I could find myself confronted with a rebel who wouldn't think twice before putting me to death.

So, when I heard the crack of gunfire and a sudden explosion, which was the norm, I flinched internally and decided to take the rough way out. I made some mental notes and figured that it was a road less travelled; hence, the possibility of running into a rebel was quite faint. As I was lost in my thoughts, I could feel another explosion that had become background noise by then, like a soundtrack of daily life. I stopped for a second, struggling with the thought of returning home.

But then it occurred to me that I had come far from home, and returning would be equally dangerous. So, my heart compelled me to move forward and leave the rest to the fate. I convinced myself that the road I was taking was safer than others. By then, my mind had already drifted to the feeling of weightlessness I always experienced when I swam. I was paying no heed to anything, but then, something caught my eye, halting me in my tracks.

At first, I thought it was just a bundle of clothes or discarded debris lying in the bushes. My eyes caught the faint movement, and curiosity got the better of me. As I stepped closer, the world seemed to slow, my heart beginning to beat louder in my chest, a primal instinct warning me that something was wrong. And then, I saw her.

A woman, her body twisted awkwardly in the dirt, lay there fighting for her life. Her breaths were shallow, her chest barely rising as blood seeped into the earth beneath her. I froze, every muscle in my body locking up as my mind tried to make sense of the scene before me. She wasn't just a random woman lying there; she was pregnant or at least, she had been.

Beside her, lying grotesquely still in the dirt, was her baby. My stomach lurched as I took in the sight. Her abdomen had been torn open. It was such a horrific sight that I felt like I would get sick. Her flesh was brutalized in a way that no words could ever truly capture. To the outside world, it might look like an attempted murder, but those who had been living in the hellhole of Liberia knew very well that it was a message, a warning. It was a cruel, unforgiving display of power and hatred, and I knew it my heart of hearts that they took pleasure in committing this grotesque crime.

The woman's eyes fluttered open for a brief moment, catching mine. I could see the pain etched into every line of her face. I could also see the desperation and the fear that was emanating from every fiber of her being. There was so much that I felt at that moment – pity for her, hate for rebels, andhelplessness for myself. It's not like I didn't want to help; I did. I wanted to do something, anything but my feet wouldn't let me; they wouldn't move. No matter how hard I tried, I couldn't move myself from that spot.

I could feel my body numbing as if paralyzed with shock, fear, and the overwhelming realization that I had stumbled upon something I was never supposed to see. Not just me. No one was supposed to see that. And more than that, no one was supposed to go through such a horror. Nobody deserved to be cut down like an animal. No one deserved to go through the atrocities these god-forsaken people were carrying out against breathing humans, let alone pregnant women.

As I was engrossed in my thoughts, urging myself to move, I saw her lips parted as if to say something, but no words came out. My heart shattered into a thousand pieces at the sight of her helplessness. She seemed so small under the weight of her condition that you could almost forget that she just had a baby. I could see her trying to say something, to move, to cling to life, but her body was giving up, and the effort was too much for her to bear.

Out of nowhere, my gaze fell on the tiny form beside her. The baby, barely there, barely surviving, barely distinguishable as a human anymore, was just lying there in its lifeless form. It was evident that it had been ripped from her womb brutally. Clearly, it was a cruel violation of both life and death. The sheer viciousness of the crime was staggering. I couldn't help but think that he was not just a random act of violence. It wasn't like that a guy just came and did this to her. If it were random, she would have been pushed or, at most, beaten for getting in the way. But no, it wasn't like that. This was a calculated move, done purposely.

Even at that moment, as I could barely move myself to approach the almost lifeless pair of mother and baby, I knew that the rebels, the tyrants that they were, tried to ensure that the woman would not survive. Life meant nothing to them. Killing, maiming, and torturing were the sole purposes of their lives, mere games for their amusements. These heinous acts were a way to satisfy their ego and their thirst for power. And this woman, who had probably been at the wrong place at the wrong time, had been their latest victim.

My mind raced, disgusted by the sheer heinousness of the crime. But more than that, I kind of felt disgusted with myself too, for not being able to do anything. I was torn between wanting to help and knowing that I couldn't. The rebels were everywhere, watching, waiting. Any sign of compassion, any attempt to intervene, could result in my own death or worse. After all, they didn't need much of an excuse to snuff out another life.

Even as I stood there, trembling, I could feel their presence. I could feel the invisible weight of their cruelty pressing down on me. I knew that speaking of what I had seen could get me killed. I knew that attempting to help right now could get me killed as well. I could easily become another body left to rot in the dirt, another grim statistic in a war that had lost its purpose long ago.

So, to my absolute shame, I did nothing. I stood there, rooted to the spot, helpless and terrified until the woman's shallow breaths slowed and eventually stopped. She was gone. The silence that followed was deafening. My heartbeat echoed in my ears as I forced myself to back away, to leave the scene behind me. My legs moved on their own, carrying me further and further away from the gruesome reality I had just witnessed.

I don't know how long I walked. Minutes? Hours? Time had lost all meaning. I couldn't get the image of that woman out of my head. It felt like the sight of her body, her baby, the sheer horror of what I had just witnessed was eating me alive. It clung to me like a second skin. It was like a constant reminder of human cruelty that we were unfortunate enough to witness.

When I finally reached home, I didn't say a word. I couldn't say a word. How could I? I was too scared, not to mention too ashamed, for leaving her there to die. Also, the fear of repercussions weighed too heavily on my chest, suffocating any words that might have come out. To speak of what I had seen would be a death sentence. In the rebel's eyes, nothing was off-limits. To them, we were nothing more than pawns in their sick game.

The silence was a prison. I wanted to scream, to cry, to tell someone, anyone, about what I had seen, but I couldn't. It weighed heavily on me. Even within the safety of my own family, I felt the need to hold it all in. The rebels had eyes and ears everywhere. We had learned to live in silence, to bury our emotions deep inside where they couldn't be used against us. But the weight of that silence took a toll.

It wasn't just me. The entire camp seemed to be under a veil of quiet despair. People moved about their daily lives with a grim determination, their faces expressionless, their eyes dull. Everyone had seen too much and experienced too much. We were all carrying our own burdens of trauma, our own memories of horror that we could never speak of. And in that silence, the fear only grew.

I knew others had witnessed similar atrocities. I had heard whispers of children stumbling upon the remains of their neighbors and of mothers finding their sons hanging from trees. But no one spoke openly about it. They knew that if they did, they would invite danger. They didn't want to invite the wrath of the rebels who patrolled our every move. So, we lived in a kind of suspended terror, always watching, always waiting, but never speaking.

The mental toll was immense. I could see it in the way people walked with their shoulders hunched and slow steps. The weight of what we were going through was too much to carry, but we had no choice. There was no escape, no reprieve from the constant fear that gnawed at our sanity. Every night, I used to be awake. I couldn't believe my own mind was playing tricks on me. It kept replaying the scene of that woman over and over again. Her face haunted my dreams. Her suffering haunted my existence.

As the days passed, I began to realize that what I had seen wasn't an isolated incident. It didn't happen that one time only. It was happening all around me, all around us. The war had turned our country into a breeding ground for violence and cruelty, and no one was safe. And honestly, nobody cared as well. The rebels moved through the land like locusts, consuming everything in their path. They didn't even care about the women, children, or the elderly. No one was spared from their brutality.

The political situation had worsened beyond anything we could have imagined. The factions that had once fought for power and control had lost all sense of purpose. Now, it was just about survival, their survival, at the expense of everyone else. They took pleasure in their cruelty, using fear as a weapon to maintain their grip on power. And it worked. We were all too afraid to stand up, too afraid to speak out.

In the weeks following that day, I heard of more incidents. People whispered about bodies being found in the fields, about women being dragged from their homes in the dead of night, never to be seen again. The horrors had become so common that we almost stopped reacting to them. It was as if we had become numb to the violence, our minds protecting us from the full weight of what was happening around us.

But even as we tried to shield ourselves from the brutality, the emotional impact lingered. It ate away at us, slowly eroding any sense of hope or humanity we had left. I could see it in my family, in the way my aunt's hands trembled when she thought no one was looking, in the way my sisters avoided eye contact, their gazes fixed firmly on the ground as they went about their daily tasks. The trauma was everywhere. It was suffocating, an invisible force that pressed down on us all, but we never spoke of it. Silence was our shield. It was our way of protecting ourselves from the terror that loomed over us.

Fear became our constant companion, lingering in every corner, every shadow, every conversation. Every step outside our home was a gamble. We lived under the constant threat of being seen, of being caught, of being accused of something, anything, that could lead to our deaths. The rebels didn't need a reason to kill; they simply did it because they could. And that power, that absolute control over life and death, was the most terrifying thing of all.

The fear wasn't just of the rebels, though. It was also the fear of what we had seen, of what we knew. The knowledge that we were living in a world where life had lost its value, where cruelty had become the norm, weighed on us like a heavy cloak. Even when I was with my family, the fear never left. We learned to communicate in hushed tones, always looking over our shoulders, always aware of the possibility that someone might be listening.

There were days when the fear felt so thick that it was hard to breathe. Every loud noise, like a door slamming or a distant shout, sent my heart racing. My body would get tensed in anticipation of the worst. I'd seen too much and knew too much to ever feel safe again. The rebels were always watching, always waiting for someone to slip up. And if you did, if you dared to defy them in any way, the consequences were swift and brutal.

I remembered a family not far from ours who had tried to escape. They had been quiet about it, of course, whispering their plans late at night when they thought no one was listening. But word had gotten out, as it always did. The rebels found out, and the family was dragged from their home in broad daylight. We all watched from behind our windows, too afraid to intervene, too afraid to even breathe. The mother had begged for mercy, but there was none to be found. The rebels made an example of them. They were shot in the street, one by one, while we watched, helpless.

That was the reality we lived in, a world where trying to escape tyranny could mean your death. But even in that terror, even in the face of such overwhelming fear, we clung to the hope that maybe, somehow, we could survive. Maybe we could find a way out.

As much as we feared the rebels, there was a kind of unspoken bond that formed between those of us who lived under their rule. We didn't talk about it; we couldn't, but we all knew. We all understood the weight of the trauma we carried, the fear that gnawed at our minds day and night. In some strange way, that shared suffering brought us closer. We moved through life together, side by side, even if we couldn't openly acknowledge the horrors we had witnessed.

There were moments, though, brief flickers of connection where someone would catch your eye, and in that look, you could see that they understood. They knew. They had seen things, too. And in that moment, you weren't alone. It didn't make the fear go away, didn't make the trauma disappear, but it reminded you that you weren't the only one. That somehow, amidst all the chaos and brutality, there were still others who were fighting to survive, just like you.

But survival came at a cost. The more we witnessed, the more we experienced, the more we had to bury inside ourselves. There was no room for grief, no time to process the trauma. If you broke down, if you let the fear consume you, you wouldn't make it. You had to be strong, even when every part of you wanted to collapse under the weight of it all. There were days when I wanted to scream, to cry, to let out the anger, fear, and grief that had built up inside me. But I couldn't. None of us could.

The trauma became a part of us, shaping who we were and how we interacted with the world. It hardened us and forced us to close off parts of ourselves that had once been open and vulnerable. Trust became a rare commodity, and even within our own families, there was a level of caution that hadn't existed before. We loved each other, yes, but the fear of betrayal, of saying the wrong thing, of being overheard always lingered in the back of our minds.

The mental toll of living under constant fear and witnessing such brutality was also immense. We were all dealing with it in our own ways, though none of us could talk about it. There were no therapists, no counselors, no safe spaces where we could unburden ourselves of the trauma. Instead, we carried it with us, letting it fester and grow inside us until it became a permanent part of who we were.

For the children, it was even worse. They were growing up in a world where violence was the norm, where the sound of gunfire and explosions was as common as birdsong. They didn't know anything else. I could see the fear in their eyes, the confusion, the way they clung to their parents, desperate for some sense of security that simply didn't exist anymore. The war had stolen their childhoods, replacing innocence with terror.

For the adults, it was a different kind of suffering. They had memories of what life had been like before the war, of a time when we didn't have to live in fear. That made it harder, in some ways. They knew what they had lost, and they grieved for it, even if they couldn't express that grief out loud.

Sleep became elusive. The nightmares were relentless. There were vivid replays of the horrors we had witnessed. I would wake up in a cold sweat, my heart pounding, the images of that pregnant woman flashing behind my eyelids. I could hear her shallow breaths and see the lifeless body of her child lying beside her. No matter how hard I tried, I couldn't escape it. And I knew I wasn't alone. My family was haunted by their own demons, their own memories of the things they had seen but couldn't speak of.

As the war dragged on, the violence escalated. The rebels grew bolder. Their brutality was more brazen. They no longer bothered to hide their atrocities. In fact, they seemed to revel in them, using fear and intimidation as tools to control us. The camp we lived in had once been a place of refuge. It was a temporary escape from the chaos of the outside world. But now, there came a time when we were not safe even there.

Rumors spread like wildfire. We heard whispers of other camps being raided, of entire families being slaughtered in their sleep. The rebels were expanding their territory, and it was only a matter of time before they came for us, which was why we decided to move. Every day felt like walking on a tightrope, balancing precariously between life and death.

We heard of a new faction, more ruthless than the last, moving closer to our camp. They were known for their cruelty, for the way they executed entire villages without mercy. The fear in the camp grew, and with it, the silence. No one spoke of the impending danger, but we all felt it. It was only a matter of time before they came for us.

That day, when I found the pregnant woman, was a turning point for me. It was as if I had come face to face with the devil himself, seen the worst of humanity laid bare in the most gruesome way possible. The war had taken so much from us already: our homes, our safety, our sense of normalcy, but that day, it took something more. It took my ability to believe in the goodness of the world.

I often thought back to the woman's face, the way her eyes had fluttered open just long enough to meet mine. There had been so much pain in those eyes, so much fear. But there had also been something else – resignation. She had known she was going to die, had known that there was no help coming, no one who could save her. And in that moment, I realized that we were all just like her. We were all fighting for survival in a world that had no mercy.

The rebels were the devil's grin. They reminded us that evil was real, and it walked among us. They thrived on our fear and fed off our suffering, and there was nothing we could do to stop them. The war had changed everything, twisted our world into something unrecognizable, something dark and terrifying. But even in that darkness, we had to keep going. We had to survive, if only because that was all we had left.

Surviving the brutality of the war came with a cost. We had to harden ourselves and close off parts of our hearts that had once been open. We had to become numb to the violence, the bloodshed, the suffering. It was the only way to keep going, to protect ourselves from the horrors we witnessed every day. But even as we built walls around our hearts, the trauma lingered. It stayed with us. It was like a shadow that followed us wherever we went. We could never forget what we had seen, what we had experienced. It shaped us and defined us, and there was no escaping it.

The war had taken so much from us already, but it hadn't taken everything. We still had each other, still had the hope that maybe, one day, we would be free from the grip of fear.

Chapter 8

The Unusual Stranger

Now that we were leaving, I couldn't help but feel a little hopeful for the future. Even though the war had thrown us all into a whirlwind of uncertainty and terror, and there was no way to be certain what the future holds for us, there was something in my heart that was telling me that things were about to get better for me and my family.

Then, there was this other side of me, the realist side, the side deeply wounded by was side, the side that was scarred for life, thanks to the atrocities it has witnessed. That side of me overpowered the hopeful streak completely. It kept warning me, urging me to be cautious. It kept reminding me that nothing good had come out of this war, and nothing would ever be worth living again. It kept reminding me of the horror I had witnessed, of the bloodshed I had heard about, of the horrific incidents I came across. But I shouted it down, of course, internally. I convinced myself to find hope in the smallest things, and then, even the smallest glimmer of hope seemed like a lifeline to my yearning heart.

Everything that was keeping us away from that godforsaken place seemed attractive, and everyone who offered us assistance seemed a godsend. It was in this context that I encountered her, an unusual woman who approached us sweetly. In that moment, she was directly sent from heaven, to get us out of the mess we found ourselves in.

Crossing the forest was not so easy. We had to go through numerous obstacles, and it was no easy feat. If you ask me the truth, we weren't even prepared properly. My aunt had gathered information, but it wasn't enough; we had to be prepared. We had to dot all the Is and cross all the Ts, but there was no time. So, we left with the little we could grab.

During that arduous journey, a lady with an unusual appearance and intriguing demeanor reached me with what seemed like a promise to offerhelp. She wasn't anyone I had ever met before, neither in Marry Camp nor in any other places we were laying low. But then there were so many people taking refuge, so it wasn't unusual for faces to blur together. Of course, the camp was crowded with people who, like us, were trying to escape the horrors of war, moving quietly through life as if trying to avoid catching the attention of the rebels.

So, when I found myself confronted by this mysterious woman, I didn't think much of it. But something surely seemed off. With a washed-up image like that of an old day and a daring authority that spoke of overconfidence, she approached me without any hesitation. Today, if I woman like that would approach me, I'd probably laud her over her confident demeanor, but back then, when everyone was skeptical and afraid, confidence was a luxury none of us could afford.

But there was something about that woman that seemed eerie, something that would keep you on the edge. There was a strange blend of authority and mystery that enthralled me, something in the way she carried herself that would surely catch the attention of anyone she'd approached. During the time when everything seemed uncertain and everyone seemed timid, she felt like a nightmare dressed like a daydream.

I was sure I didn't know her personally neither did I ever see her. Yet, there was an unnerving familiarity about her. To tell you the truth, it made me a little uncomfortable. But at that moment, she seemed like she was desperate. So, I pushed my discomfort aside. I gave myself a pep talk, saying that in a war-torn camp, I must step up and ensure older people are taken care of. Since she was an old lady and respect for elders was still deeply ingrained in me, I couldn't refuse her. Refusing to help someone who looked like they needed assistance was unthinkable at that moment.

"Could you help me carry my load to the other side of the camp?" she asked, her voice steady but low as if she didn't want to attract unnecessary attention. I was cautious, too, not wanting to get highlighted. There were very few people that we had met on our way who, like us, were trying to escape the tyranny. Still, we could trust no one, and we could get detected easily.

Very slowly, I moved ahead and whispered a silent yes to her. It almost seemed like I agreed without a second thought. Even though my discomfort was quite evident, I figured that we were all trying to survive in whatever way we could, and helping others was the decent thing to do. However I could help, in whatever small ways, I was ready. It was one of the few things that still connected us to our humanity.

So I picked up her load. It was a collection of belongings, which were packed haphazardly, scattered around into a tattered sack. It wasn't too heavy, so she could have held it on her own without requiring help. But there was something in the way she asked me that I couldn't voice my thoughts. Not to mention, I thought it would be extremely rude.

Picking up her sack, I followed the old lady. We made our way to a small, dimly lit house on the edge of the camp. While we were walking, I noticed that the moon was hanging low in the sky, casting long shadows over the camp.

There was something so beautiful, so terrifying about the moon that day. It was shining brightly, too brightly for my liking, honestly.

Usually, I loved looking at the full moon. It reminded me that there was still a shining light in my life, that no matter what happens, its shine would remain. But that day, it was almost too bright. I'd look up, and it would feel like its shine would pierce through my eyes, warning me that everything that shines is gold.

Honestly, if you ask me that truth, it was the kind of night that felt ominous, as if something was lurking just out of sight, waiting for the right moment to strike. Something that would eat me alive.

Something that was waiting for me to take the wrong step. But by that time, I had been habitual of looking over my shoulder and expecting the worse. So, when everything about that warned me, I ignored it and moved forward. When we reached the house, she turned to me and smiled, a smile that, in retrospect, felt more like a mask than a gesture of gratitude.

"Why don't you come inside for a moment?" she asked, her tone taking on an oddly suggestive edge that immediately made me uncomfortable. I hesitated, suddenly unsure of myself. Tradition demanded respect for elders, especially women, and in normal circumstances, entering her house would have been seen as an innocent act of kindness. But something about the way she asked felt wrong like there was an unspoken implication behind her words.

I refused at first, muttering something about needing to get back to my family. But she persisted, and before I knew it, I found myself stepping inside the house. I felt like my reluctance was overshadowed by her persistence. At that time, I convinced myself that I was burdened under the weight of cultural expectations, but I knew in my heart of hearts it wasn't just that. Her house was a simple dwelling, not much different from the others in the camp. It was bare and worn down by the ravages of war, with little more than the essentials to keep someone alive. She led me to a small room and gestured for me to sit.

"You've been working hard," she said, her voice soft but insistent. "You need to rest."

Again, I refused, but she wouldn't take no for an answer. Before I could fully process what was happening, she led me out of the house, behind it, to a tree where the moonlight barely reached. The air was thick with tension, and I felt my heart begin to race. Something wasn't right. It happened so fast that, even now, it feels like a blur. She spread a blanket on the ground, and before I could react, she made her move. At first, it was just small touches, touches that seemed harmless at first, but as time went by, they carried with them a weight of something much darker. She started touching me. Her hands lingered longer than they should have, and the way she looked at me made my stomach churn.

Fear gripped me. I tried to pull away, but she was insistent. She was making sexual advances at me, something I had never experienced before, even in the wartorn state. She forced me to sit on the blanket she had laid out on the ground and pinned me to the ground. She sat on me with such ferocity that I lost my balance.

It was such a strange feeling like something inside me was asking me to run. But there was nothing I could do. I felt helpless beyond measure. As she grew bolder and more invasive, my mind raced with confusion and panic. I didn't know what to do. On one hand, I was terrified of offending her, of disrespecting an elder in a culture where such acts could have severe consequences. On the other hand, I felt an overwhelming sense of revulsion and fear at what was happening.

Before I knew it, I had succumbed to her demands, not out of desire but out of a complex mix of fear and helplessness. It was as though the world had shrunk down to that moment, that place under the tree, with only the moonlight as witness to what was happening. I felt paralyzed. I was trapped in a situation that made no sense but was terrifyingly real.

When it was over, I left her house in a daze, my mind racing with a thousand thoughts, none of which made sense. I couldn't process what had just happened. I felt dirty, confused, and ashamed. More than anything, I felt stuck. There was something so carnal, so sinister about her stance that I felt like I had been diminished as a person. I felt so ashamed, so embarrassed that I couldn't tell anyone. What if she was connected to the rebels? What if she was someone's wife, sister, or girlfriend? What if saying something led to even more violence, not only for me but for my family?

The fear of retaliation was so overwhelming that I didn't even consider confiding in anyone. I wanted to, I really did, but I couldn't being myself to. I was terrified like never before. I had felt scared before, sure, but now, it was something else. Something much, much worse. In a camp where death was a constant companion and survival hinged on keeping your head down, telling someone about the incident seemed like a death sentence. So, I stayed silent.

The days that followed were a blur of emotions I couldn't fully understand. I tried to push the memory of that night out of my mind, but it lingered. It felt so dirty, as if someone or something had marked me, stamping me dirty for life. It felt like a dark cloud was hovering over me, no matter what I did. I threw myself into helping my family, into planning our escape, into anything that would keep my mind occupied. But the memory was always there, always at the back of my mind, lurking in the background, gnawing at me. I would be swamped with work, and there it would be, knocking at the door of my tarnished heart, smiling its sinister smile, challenging me to escape it.

The incident left scars that I didn't fully understand at the time. To the outside world, it might be just a physical act; however, to me, who had gone through it, it was the manipulation, the sense of powerlessness, and the violation of trust that haunted me in ways I couldn't articulate. The moments that should have felt safe and secure, the ones where I should have felt in control, were instead tainted by a sense of vulnerability and confusion.

I remember trying to make sense of everything, trying to piece it all together, telling myself that it did not happen or it wasn't as bad as I felt. But nothing seemed to fit. There was nothing I could tell myself that would make me feel better. When it happened, I was disgusted by her and by myself. But the aftermath was so, so much worse. I couldn't get it out of my head. The echoes of betrayal that lingered in the corners of my mind were very much there, even after the physical pain of it had faded.

What truly unsettled me was the psychological toll. I began to question myself, to wonder if I had somehow brought it on, even though I knew deep down that I hadn't. There were moments when doubt crept in. There were moments when I wondered if I had done something to invite it if I had been too trusting, too naive, too unaware. I replayed every interaction, searching for signs I might have missed, things I could have done differently. And in doing so, I lost sight of the fact that the blame didn't belong to me. I kept blaming myself when it was never mine to carry. But in those early days, it felt easier to believe that I was somehow complicit, that there was something I had done to deserve it.

What really surprised me was the manipulation of the situation, of her. It was subtle but pervasive. It wasn't just about what she did to me on purpose, it was the way it made me doubt my own instincts, my own worth. I felt so worthless that I limited my contact and didn't talk to anyone for several days. My family members kept asking me what was wrong, but I couldn't bring myself to voice it out.

I had always prided myself on being strong, on knowing my boundaries, but suddenly, everything felt blurry. The violation of trust was too much to bear. The fact that someone I had once trusted had taken advantage of that trust in the most intimate way was too much to stomach. It was a betrayal of everything I thought I understood about people, about relationships, about my own safety.

In the days and weeks that followed, I felt like I was living in a fog. On the outside, I tried to keep things together, pretending that everything was fine, even though inside, I was a mess. I smiled when I had to keep up appearances, but I was unraveling in ways I didn't know how to fix. I didn't know how to explain the feeling of being so utterly unmoored, of having a part of me taken that I didn't even know how to get back.

The hardest part was reconciling the two versions of myself: the person I had been before the incident and the person I had become afterward. There was a gap between those versions of me, a chasm that I didn't know how to cross. I wanted to believe that I was still the same person, but the truth was that I was changed. The way I viewed the world, the way I viewed myself, had shifted. The innocence I once had, the confidence that came with it, had been stripped away. And even though I knew, on some level, that I had done nothing wrong, the weight of the experience made it hard to escape the feeling that I had somehow failed, somehow let myself down.

I think the hardest part of all was learning to trust myself again, to understand that I wasn't broken, that I hadn't failed, and that I deserved the same compassion I would offer anyone else in my position. It took time, much longer than I anticipated, but eventually, I began to heal. It wasn't something that happened overnight, and it certainly wasn't easy, but slowly, I started to reclaim the pieces of myself that I thought I had lost forever. And though the scars remain, they are no longer the defining feature of who I am. They are part of me, yes, but they no longer define me.

But boy, oh, boy. The psychological toll was immense. I found it harder to trust people, especially women. Every interaction felt like a potential threat, and I started to pull away from the people around me. Even when we finally made it to Monrovia, and life settled into a more peaceful routine, the memory of that night followed me like a shadow. It affected my relationships, making it difficult for me to connect with others on a deeper level. I kept people at a distance, afraid of being hurt, afraid of being manipulated again.

For years, I stayed silent about what had happened. It wasn't until much later that I finally confided in someone, and even then, the weight of the experience hadn't lessened. It was a burden I had carried alone for so long that sharing it felt almost impossible.

What happened to me wasn't an isolated incident. Sexual harassment, manipulation, and assault are global issues that affect millions of people, especially those in vulnerable situations. War zones, refugee camps, and places of displacement create an environment where predators can thrive, exploiting the fear and chaos to take advantage of those who are already suffering.

Displaced people, in particular, are at a higher risk of sexual harassment and assault. When governments fail to protect their citizens, when people are forced to flee their homes and live in temporary camps, the structures that normally provide safety and accountability crumble. In these situations, the most vulnerable, women, children, and the displaced, are often the ones who suffer the most.

The incident with the unusual woman opened my eyes to the harsh realities of sexual exploitation in times of war. It was a personal reminder of how predators can use power dynamics and fear to manipulate and control others and how, in situations of extreme vulnerability, even those who seem trustworthy can turn out to have ulterior motives.

The psychological impact of sexual harassment and assault is profound, not just for those who experience it but for society as a whole. It creates a culture of fear, silence, and shame, where victims feel too afraid to speak out, and perpetrators are rarely held accountable. This is especially true in conflict zones, where law and order have broken down, and survival is the primary concern.

The trauma of such experiences can last a lifetime, affecting relationships, self-esteem, and mental health. For those who have been displaced by war or conflict, the added trauma of sexual harassment or assault compounds the already overwhelming stress of losing your home, family, and sense of security.

In my case, the encounter with the unusual woman left lasting scars. It shaped the way I viewed relationships, trust, and power. Even as I moved on with my life, even as I found peace in Monrovia and eventually immigrated to the United States, the memory of that night stayed with me. It was a reminder of the darkness that can exist even in the most unexpected places.

It took years for me to fully process what had happened, and even now, the memory is painful. But sharing my story has helped me begin the healing process. It's a reminder that, no matter how dark the circumstances, we must find the strength to confront our trauma and seek justice, not just for ourselves but for all those who have been silenced by fear.

Chapter 9

The Good Part

We have seen numerous struggles in Liberia, more than I can count on my fingers. The constant struggle crushed our hearts, our spirits time and time again. But it wasn't all bad. Until we were in Marry Camp, we were constantly under threat. But we did not give up. We never backed down. We never let anyone dampen our will to live. We wanted to live, and we did everything in our power to leave that godforsaken place and start anew. And that's how we decided to move to Monrovia – the capital of Liberia.

Even though it wasn't completely safe, there were security threat there as well, but it wasn't as bad as it was back at Marry Camp. Such campsites were heavily guarded by rebels as they relished in the pain of those who had no means, no resources. The use to target the weak and thoroughly enjoyed their downfall. But things were different in the capital. Things were somewhat better, and rebels were somewhat tamed down.

Hence, Monrovia seemed like a viable option. After years of living in fear and uncertainty and facing displacements numerous times, it was our right to get to choose a place that could often us a semblance of peace and quiet. We were prepared for the ambiguity of the situation; it was much better than the decided tyranny with no accountability.

After an incredibly difficult journey, we finally made it to Monrovia. It was a road less travelled, fraught with obstacles and problems. We faced many issues that broke our backs. It wasn't easy moving along various villages and protecting ourselves from the wrath of the rebels. However, my mother and aunt strategized together and we kids followed route. We never questioned their judgement, never let them down. We did what we were told, and finally got a reward – a seamless move to a new place where we could finally breathe without having to watch our backs.

When we stepped in Monrovia, I felt its air in my bones. There was something about it, probably the freedom that had been missing from our lives for many, many years. It was the first real glimpse of hope we had seen in a long time. We knew that we weren't completely safe there, too, far from it in fact, but still, it was way better than Marry Camp and the atrocities that we faced there.

I remember feeling a sense of stability there, not completely, but it was indeed a possibility. We could finally rebuild our lives there, a life we weren't afraid to live, a life where no one would deliberately steal from us. If I tell you the truth, the city was a far cry from the terrorfilled villages and camps we had been forced to pass through. It felt like a sanctuary, even though the war had left its scars here too.

Even when we were living there, I couldn't forget how truly difficult it really had been for us. We knew that the rebels had still controlled much of the surrounding areas, and we had to be careful. I used ot have nightmares about the traumatic journey we had. We were constantly stressed about getting detected. I'd often dream of getting captured. Since it was very much a possibility, it was constantly hovering over our heads. I'd wake up sweating, as if it was really happening to me.

But then I'd look out my window and see the city come alive. Instead of the constant crackle of gunfire and the shuddering blasts I had grown used to, I heard the roar of engines, the hum of everyday life. The urban landscape was nothing like the war-torn reality I had known. I'd watch small markets spring up, vibrant with activity, and it felt almost like a dream to my bruised heart, so far removed from the devastation I'd lived through. Every time a car passed by, the sound of its engine would make my pulse quicken. It would remind me of a life I could barely imagine back at Marry Camp.

The people in the streets moved with such ease, such freedom, that I couldn't help but feel a deep ache in my chest. They walked without fear, without that heavy weight of worry always pressing down on them. They were free, their minds were light, and their hearts were unburdened, and you could see that. You could feel it in the way they moved. I would see families strolling down the sidewalks, people laughing with friends, the elderly chatting outside cafes, and it was as though they carried a purpose that I could only envy. They weren't aimless, only thinking about saving their necks, they were living, truly living. There was no hurry in their steps, no quick glances over their shoulders. They moved through the city with such a natural grace, like they knew exactly who they were and where they were going.

I longed to feel that sense of certainty, that peace of mind. I wanted to know what it was like to breathe without fear. It wasn't resentment that I felt, it was more like a quiet envy, a longing for a life I could have had if I had been born here, in this city, under different skies. It was a place where people had purpose, where they moved through their days with a confidence that seemed foreign to my aching, bruised, war-stricken heart.

To me, an outsider, it felt like the city was waking from a long sleep, struggling to shake off the chaos of war, but that wasn't the case. It had always been way better than the camp sides. Now that we were living there, it felt like a weight had been lifted from my shoulders.

With all the envy, I was also thankful. At least we were way better than other who had been executed. We had survived the journey, and now, for the first time in a long while, we could start to dream of a future again.

And it wasn't like we had it easy here. It was difficult to get accustomed with the rules, regulations, and intricacies of the urban life. We had been habitual of living in a simple environment where whatever little we had or whatever little we did had been enough for us. But now that we were living in the city where life was hard and fast, it was harder for us to catch up. We had to give up our habits and adapt to the new environment. We had no one to guide us, no one to put our mind as ease, no one to hold our hand and drag us forward. We had to make do on our own.

Yet, I'd be lying if I said it wasn't working in our favor. Like I said, things were way better than back at Marry Camp. We could breath, eat, sleep, move about without anyone's fear. We had a certain level of autonomy that had been missing my entire life. Nobody was out to kill us just for the fun of it. For a while, we lived in the relative peace of the city, adjusting to life in an environment that wasn't ruled by immediate violence. It wasn't perfect, but it was enough, way better what we had ever imagined.

If you ask me about my personal experience, I'd say Monrovia was the first place I felt like me, the person that I wanted to be. It was the place where I began to build myself. It was a place where I finally had the chance to start working on my life, a life where I would have my own identity, where I wouldn't be just another statistic. Here, I had opportunities to get out of my shell and make a man out of myself, a man who wasn't afraid to live, a man who wasn't afraid to dream.

So, once we settled there, I started looking within. "What was I most passionate about?" I'd ask myself. And every time I did, I would only be confronted with only one answer– Music. I knew in my heart of hearts that music was my true calling.

Whenever I thought about a future, I'd see myself holding a guitar rocking the stage. It was something that gave me immense pleasure, like I could feel myself getting away from the horrors of the world, finding solace in the beat of the music. No matter what was happening in my life, I had always been drawn towards it. All I'd want to do at the end of the day would make my own tunes and dance to them, forgetting everything from the outside world. I can safely say that it was something that sustained me throughout the hardest times.

Luckily, an opportunity presented itself that gave me a chance to realize my dream. A neighbor asked me if I would like to join gospel music industry. I was shocked beyond measure. I had always loved getting involved in everything musical, but I never thought I would be so lucky to be able to join the music industry professionally, that too in a safe place where I wouldn't have to look over my shoulder every minute. It was a dream come true.

And you know what was the best part? It wouldn't have to think about getting my hands dirty because god's word was included in the mix. I had been an advocate of incorporating faith into your life ever since I was a child. Even when I was stuck in our camp with gunshots reverberating our very existence, I would always believe that there was a higher power that would make things better one day. And I was right, it did. There was no way for me to no believe.

I never had any qualms about music but now I no reason to turn it down. I felt like God was trying to give me a sign, a sign to redo it all and rebuild my life as I see fit. A sign to let the past go and start afresh. A sign to embrace the serenity of my present and turn it into something meaningful for my future. So, without thinking twice, I grabbed the opportunity with both hands.

When I started my job, I was over the moon. I had never felt as purposeful as I felt there. I finally realized that true happiness comes when you put your heart and soul into something, when you don't have to worry about anything but your work, when you wake up in the morning with an agenda to do well. No matter what you do or what designation you work at, as long as your purpose drives you, you are good to go.

I worked hard and became a musical director for my church's choir. I thought about nothing but work and poured everything I had into it. Anyone who would see me say that I was obsessed. Maybe I was.

Maybe it was a way for me to heal, to find meaning again after the horrors I had seen at such a young age. Music gave me a sense of resolve, a sense of persistence, a way to connect with others and with God. It gave me power to articulate myself but I couldn't find the right words to. Pursuing music as a career felt like the start of something better, something worth holding onto.

As life in Monrovia stabilized, I couldn't help but think of the future. I was grateful for the opportunities I had in Monrovia but I didn't want to limit myself. I didn't want to get stuck in one place. I didn't want to be static in my career trajectory. I wanted to do something better, somewhere better. I wanted to challenge myself and make myself capable enough to leave it all behind. I wanted to rise from the ashes and sore high, and I wasn't going to let anything stop me.

I had always dreamed of something bigger, something beyond the confines of war-torn Liberia. So, I thought about switching places and trying my luck in the United States. We had all always heard that the US was the place to realize your dreams. It was the land of opportunities. It was the magnet attracting me to try my luck. No matter what I did, I couldn't ditch the itch to move there. The idea of pursuing the American Dream became a fantasy. In fact, it became more than that; it became a goal. I wanted more for myself, and I wanted more for my future family. The war had taken so much from us, but it hadn't taken away my desire to succeed, to build a life that was free from fear and filled with opportunity.

Eventually, that dream began to take shape. I made the move to the United States, filled with a mixture of excitement and trepidation. It was a chance to start over, to leave the pain and trauma of the past behind. But it wasn't going to be easy. Moving to the U.S. was like stepping into a different world. Everything was bigger, faster, and more complex than anything I had ever known. The culture shock was immense, and there were moments when I felt completely out of place.

But despite the challenges, I knew that this was where I wanted to be. The promise of the American Dream, of education, of opportunity, of a life where my children could grow up without the constant threat of violence was worth whatever struggles came my way.

The early years in the United States were a whirlwind of hard work and adjustment. I found a job in manufacturing, working long hours to make ends meet while also attending school. It was exhausting, but the determination to build a better life kept me going. I juggled classes and work, often finding myself studying late into the night after long shifts at the factory. There were days when I felt like giving up, but the thought of what I had escaped in Liberia, and what I wanted to achieve, pushed me forward.

My first job in the US was with a manufacturing company, where I worked as a Manufacturing Technician. It wasn't glamorous work, pretty hard for a newbie, but it was steady, and it gave me the chance to learn valuable skills. Over time, I began to climb the ranks, gaining more responsibilities and earning the respect of my colleagues. But as much as I appreciated the opportunities manufacturing offered, I knew that I wanted more. I wanted to make a real difference in my life and the lives of others.

It wasn't long before I decided to shift my focus. I went back to school. I was determined to expand my academic and professional portfolio. I knew that education was the key to unlocking greater opportunities, and I wasn't going to let the hardships of the past hold me back. As I studied, I continued to work, balancing the demands of both in a constant effort to better myself and provide for my future family.

Life in the US was nothing like what I had experienced growing up. The sheer scale of everything was overwhelming. From the sprawling cities to the constant rush of people and technology, it felt like the world was moving at a speed that was unfamiliar to me. I wasn't used to going that fast or thinking that quickly. I was only familiar with a fight or flight response. That was my go to. That was what I accustomed with. My life had always been slower; it had personal quality to it. I wasn't used to putting myself out there. If anything, I was always told to hide myself, to keep my head down, and to stay out of the spotlight. But here, everything was different. Everything was completely opposite. Everyone only seemed focused on productivity and success, and I'm not ashamed to say that there were times when I struggled to keep up.

The thing that shocked me the most was cultural differences. In Liberia, community was everything. People looked out for each other, and there was a strong sense of shared responsibility. But in the US, nobody cared for anybody. They had a view that life was so fast that if they stopped for anyone, they'd be left behind. Hence, the emphasis was on individualism. People were more focused on their own lives, their own careers, their own personal successes. It took some time to adjust to this new way of thinking. There were moments when I felt isolated, disconnected from the world around me. I always motivated myself to keep going on. I always reminded myself that giving up was not an option. I had worked hard to reach here and there was no way that I could get succumb by the overwhelming burden of business. Over time, I learned to get settled in this new culture. I found a balance between my African roots and my new American life.

As I settled into life in the US, my career began to take off. After years of hard work in the manufacturing industry, I found myself at a crossroads. I had gained valuable experience, but I knew that I wanted to do something more meaningful, something that would have a greater impact on the world. That's when I made the decision to transition into the pharmaceutical industry.

This new direction opened up a world of opportunities. Working in the pharmaceutical sector allowed me to be part of something larger than myself, to contribute to the creation of products that could improve people's lives. It was a rewarding experience, one that gave me a sense of fulfillment and purpose that I hadn't felt in my previous roles. I continued to pursue my education, determined to stay ahead of the curve and continue growing both personally and professionally.

The transition wasn't easy. Learning the ins and outs of a new industry took time, and there were plenty of challenges along the way. But I had always been determined, and I approached this new chapter of my life with the same resilience that had carried me through the war and the early days in the US Over time, I began to excel in my new role, earning the respect of my peers and building a reputation as someone who could be counted on to get the job done.

By that time, I was settled enough to focus on my personal life as well. My mother was constantly worried for me. She wanted me to build a family of my own, someone I could call mine. I was so engrossed in my work that didn't think about anything. But one thing was sure, fatherhood was always something I had dreamed of. The only thing that held me back was my hesitancy. The trauma I had didn't let me shoulder such a big responsibility for a long time. I was hesitant at first. My encounter with the unusual woman back in Marry Camp had left me with scars that I hadn't fully addressed. For a long time, I avoided serious relationships, afraid of what might happen if I allowed myself to become too vulnerable. But as time went on, I realized that I couldn't let the past control my future.

In 2005, my first son was born, and in that moment, everything changed. The joy I felt was overwhelming. Fatherhood was everything I had imagined it would be, and more. I wanted to give my son the best life possible, to provide him with opportunities that I had never had. It was this desire that pushed me to continue my education, to work harder than ever before, to make sure that I could give him a future filled with possibilities.

Over the years, my family grew. I became the proud father of five boys, each one bringing their own unique joy and challenges into my life. Even though I loved every bit of it, fatherhood wasn't always easy, especially as I balanced work, school, and the demands of raising a family. But it was the most rewarding thing I had ever done. Watching my boys grow, seeing them take their first steps, hearing their laughter gave me a sense of purpose that nothing else in life could.

Two of my sons have already gone on to pursue higher education, one in college and the other in technical school. The rest are still in school, and I couldn't be prouder of the young men they are becoming. My past experiences, both the good and the bad, have shaped the way I raise my children. I teach them about resilience, about the importance of education, about the value of hard work. I always tell them to stand by the right no matter how difficult things get. Most of all, I teach them to never give up, no matter what challenges life throws their way.

Now whenever I think back, my entire life flashes right before my eyes. Every horror, every trauma, everything that I went through reminds of the person that I have become. I remember everything form the war-torn villages of Liberia to the bustling cities of the United States. Even though things haven't been easy, I can't help but feel a sense of gratitude. Life hasn't always been fair to me, but it has been filled with opportunities for growth, for learning, for healing. The road I've traveled has been long and winding, but it has led me to a place of stability, of hope, of love.

I've built a life that I'm proud of, a career that has allowed me to make a difference, and a family that fills my heart with joy every single day. The challenges of the past are still there, lingering in the background, but they no longer define me. I am more than my trauma, more than the hardships I have faced. I am a father, a husband, a professional, and most of all, a survivor.

The good part of my story is that I have come out the other side stronger than ever. I have achieved my dream and I am glad they weren't handed to me. I worked hard to achieve them. I fought for everything I have today. And as I look toward the future, I know that there is still so much more to achieve, so much more to experience. The journey continues, but for now, I'm content with the life I've built, the life I've fought so hard to create for myself and my family.

Chapter 10

Perfect Timing

What makes your life worth living? Success. Now, the definition of success differs from person to person. Some people associate it with material gains, others with a healthy lifestyle. Some may think having your loved ones close to you is the true meaning of success. Others might associate it with power and authority. Whatever it means to you, one thing is for sure: it is never an easy road.

To achieve success, you must have dedication, hard work, and belief that no matter how difficult life becomes, you can overcome any challenge. You must ensure every step you take, every path you choose, and every route you go leads you to your destination, to your purpose. You must have a clear goal in your head and stick to it, regardless of the circumstances.

I did the same thing. I didn't let my past get to me. I didn't sit and wait and cry because I had a troubled childhood. I didn't make excuses to be lousy just because things didn't get my way. Instead, I worked through my trauma and took everything life threw at me in strides. I accepted my past for it was and prepared myself to work through my issues. I harbored a "go with the flow" mindset without wallowing over my horrific past.

Was it easy? No. Was it worth it? Yes, absolutely.

I won't say that it was a piece of cake that one day, I just moved to Monrovia and got on with my life. I am not saying that the transformation happened overnight or that I had a positive attitude since day one. I have had my fair share of bad days. Days when I was frustrated beyond measure, days when I didn't want to get out of bed, days when I wondered whether moving here was worth the pain. I have struggled with confidence issues not wanting to bond or get attached to anyone. I have been scared of intimacy, not wanting to get exploited once again. I have been scared to ruffle feathers at work, not wanting to attract unnecessary attention to myself.

All this while, there was a part inside me that wasn't satisfied, a part that wasn't ever happy. So, very early on, I realized I had to make some changes in the way I conduct myself. I had to change my perspective, and I knew it. So, that's what I did.

Every hardship I faced, every moment of struggle, was laying the foundation for the life I lead today. And I am so glad I took the initiative and didn't conform to the standards of society. I put my blood and sweat in and worked day in and day out. And thanks to that, I got to achieve the position of Senior Biotechnician at a reputable pharmaceutical company.

It was a milestone, not just for me but for my entire family. They all were ecstatic beyond measure. They could only imagine the kind of life the role brought for them. For somebody who has spent their entire life getting displaced, having a comfortable life with a stable income is a big deal. The perks that came with the job were everything I could never have imagined. The changes we got to experience soon after my career took over were immaculate, beyond our imagination.

Everything that changed, every transformation I had, showed me and my family how far we had come and how much we could still achieve. Once you get a sense of accomplishment, you realize that there is no limit to what you can do. The sky is the limit. The same thing happened to me. But it also reminded me that with hard work, perseverance, and the right mindset, you can do anything you set your mind to. All you have to do is take the initiative and keep at it until you achieve what you want.

But let me tell you, nothing ever comes to you in your comfort zone. You have to keep moving, keep going after it. Even after you're challenged, even after you fail. My journey to becoming a Senior Biotechnician certainly didn't happen overnight. It was a gradual climb that started with years of education, late nights, and a relentless work ethic. I had always known that education would be the key to unlocking new opportunities. When I first moved to the United States, I juggled working long shifts in manufacturing jobs while attending school. It was stressful, exhausting, and, at times, overwhelming, but I never allowed myself to give up.

I remember the pressure of balancing the demands of work, school and providing for my growing family. There were moments when I wondered if it was all worth it. But I had a vision. I wanted more than just a job; I wanted a career where I could make a difference and where I could use my skills and knowledge to impact the world in a positive way. That vision kept me going through the toughest times.

The lessons I learned from my struggles shaped me. They taught me resilience and the power of persistence. When I faced obstacles, I didn't let them break me. Instead, I used them as stepping stones, knowing that every hurdle was an opportunity to grow stronger. The sacrifices I made, the nights I spent studying after a long shift, and the countless times I pushed myself beyond my limits all contributed to the success I achieved later on.

Finally, after years of dedication, I landed a job at a pharmaceutical company. It was a position that I had worked so hard for, a reward for the effort I had put in. I was so happy, but I also equipped myself to excel at it. Mediocrity was out of the question. I had to work my way up, learning everything I could proving myself time and time again. Eventually, I earned the title of Senior Biotechnician, a role that brought stability, recognition, and fulfillment into my life. It felt like I had finally made it.

As I mentioned, my career success d idn't just affect me; it transformed my family life. Before I reached this point, we were always hustling to make ends meet. I worked several jobs, and my wife and I sacrificed a lot to provide for our boys. But with this new position came a sense of security. We no longer had to worry about whether the bills would be paid on time or whether we could afford the things our children needed.

More than the financial benefits, the job allowed me to spend more quality time with my family. I wasn't always working late nights or running between jobs just to keep us afloat. I could be there for my sons, to watch them grow, to help with their education, and to teach them the values I had learned throughout my life. My success at work allowed me to be the father I always wanted to be, the father I never had to grow up with.

And being a good father means imparting the right knowledge to your kids. Even as we reached a more comfortable life, I made sure to instill in my children the same values that had brought me to this point. I taught them about the importance of hard work, integrity, and perseverance. I wanted them to know that success doesn't come easy and that nothing in life is handed to you. You have to fight for it, just as I had fought for my career and for their future.

As I am writing this, I am reminded of a quote: "The race is not to the swift but to those that endure to the end." It's a saying I heard often during my childhood, but its meaning truly became clear through my life experiences. In a world that often celebrates quick success, it's easy to forget that true achievement is a marathon, not a sprint. It's about staying the course, even when the road is difficult, and the finish line seems impossibly far away. It's about putting your best foot forward even when things don't go in your favor. It's about knowing when to take a step back and when you initiate. Waiting for a while does not make you weak; you just have to wait for the right moment and keep at it.

I still believe perseverance was the key. There were times when it felt like everything, and everyone was against me when it would have been easier to give up. But I didn't. I kept moving forward, step by step, and eventually, I found myself in a place where I could finally be comfortable. Perseverance is what made me stand tall in the face of adversity over and over again. It's what allowed me to overcome every obstacle in my path and reach the success I now enjoy every day.

This lesson is one I hope everyone can incorporate into their own lives. No matter what your goal is, whether it's in your career, your personal life, or even your education, remember that it's not about how quickly you achieve it. It's about your ability to keep going when things get tough. Life is unpredictable, and challenges will come, but if you stay determined, there is nothing you cannot overcome.

The values of hard work and perseverance didn't just help me climb the corporate ladder; they also empowered me to take a bold step forward in my career. As much as I loved my role as a Senior Biotechnician, I knew that I wanted more. I wanted the freedom to create something of my own, to build a business that would reflect the lessons I had learned and the values I held dear.

With that in mind, I took the leap into entrepreneurship. I became a business owner, and even though the transition seemed challenging at first, it was exciting to my career – driven mind. Owning a business came with its own set of obstacles, but I approached it with the same mindset that had guided me throughout my career: hard work, resilience, and a refusal to give up. The skills I had gained in the pharmaceutical industry and the lessons I had learned throughout my life all contributed to the success of my business.

As a business owner, I had more control over my time, which allowed me to balance my professional achievements with my personal life. I could be present for my family, support my children in their education, and spend more time enjoying the fruits of my labor. It was the ultimate reward for years of hard work.

One of the most important lessons I've learned throughout my journey is the importance of balance. Success in your career is important, but it's not everything. True fulfillment comes from finding a balance between your professional achievements and your personal life. For me, that balance came in the form of my family.

Being a father of five boys has been one of the greatest joys of my life, and no amount of career success could ever replace the happiness I feel watching them grow into young men.

No doubt, my career gave me the means to provide for my family, but it was the values I instilled in my children that I consider my greatest legacy. I want my sons to know that they can achieve anything they set their minds to, just as I did. But I also want them to understand that success isn't just about money or status. It's about living a life of purpose, one that is grounded in love, integrity, and balance.

At this point, when I am able to write this book and impart wisdom to some young minds, I am filled with gratitude for all that I have accomplished, thanks to the positive mindset I have always tried to master. The road wasn't easy, but every struggle, every hardship was important. These things lead you to your destination. I have built a successful career, created a thriving business, and raised a family that I am incredibly proud of. There is nothing more I could have asked for, and there is nothing more that I want for myself. The only thing that still drives me is getting my story across. Even if only one person could learn from my story, get inspired, and get his life back on track because of it, I'd think I have fulfilled my purpose.

At this stage of my life, I can proudly say that I have endured, I have succeeded, and I will continue to inspire those who follow in my footsteps.